The American Revolution

An Enthralling Overview of the American Revolutionary War and Its Impact on the History of the United States of America

Free limited time bonus

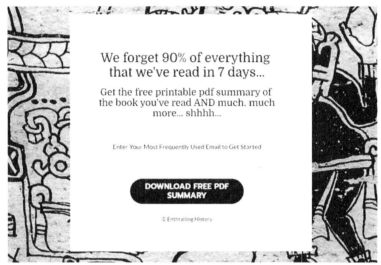

Stop for a moment. We have a free bonus set up for you. The problem is this: we forget 90% of everything that we read after 7 days. Crazy fact, right? Here's the solution: we've created a printable, 1-page pdf summary for this book that you're reading now. All you have to do to get your free pdf summary is to go to the following website: https://livetolearn.lpages.co/enthrallinghistory/

Or, Scan the QR code!

Once you do, it will be intuitive. Enjoy, and thank you!

Table of Contents

Introduction

The American Revolution is best described as the impossible dream that came true. Before the American Revolution, it was inconceivable that an army primarily made up of farmers and tradesmen could go up against the best navy and army in the world and come out the winner. The story of this American epoch continues to fascinate people to this day.

The American Revolution merits our study and appreciation. After all, the Treaty of Paris in 1783 resulted in what would become one of the largest and most powerful countries in the world: the United States of America. The revolution can also be considered an evolution in society and the rights of man. What this conflict generated inspired others and continues to be a source of reference for political scientists and historians.

We will be looking at the origins, the battles, and the compromises and decisions that led to the American Revolution and the colonists' independence. There will be instances when the reader will become enthused, and there will be times when some depression sets in. Not everything that happened during the American Revolution was sensational or the right thing to do. People made mistakes, but fortunately, they learned from most of those errors.

We want to introduce people to the American Revolution in the hope that it will spark their interest so much that they will continue reading about it. There is so much to know regarding the decisions and the actions that occurred, especially since the results remain with us. The more we understand the American Revolution, the more we will appreciate the consequences that have shaped the country Americans live in today and the world at large.

Chapter 1: Prelude to a Revolt

<u>Colonial Commerce</u>

The Thirteen Colonies in British North America were a rich and diverse basket of activity. They were not reliant on one cash crop, and the regions had distinct economies. These colonies were not centers of gold like Mexico or contained silver caches like Peru, but they were still a source of wealth and opportunity.

Agriculture served as the cornerstone of the colonies' economies, with each region specializing in crops suited to its environment. The New England colonies, whose people grappled with rocky terrain and a harsh climate, primarily engaged in subsistence farming, complemented by fishing, whaling, and timber harvesting. They capitalized on the natural resources at hand. In contrast, the Middle Colonies, which were blessed with fertile soil and a milder climate, emerged as the "breadbasket" of the Thirteen Colonies, producing surpluses of wheat, barley, and oats, feeding not only the local population but also those abroad.

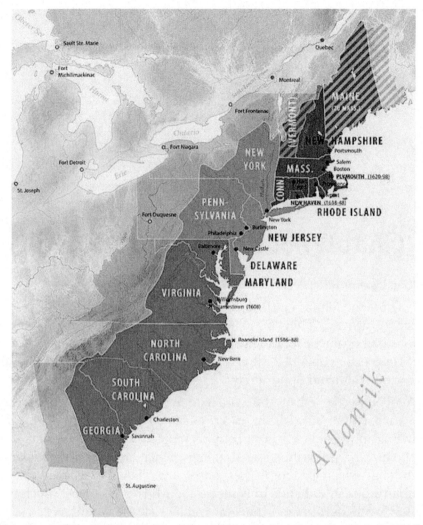

A look at the Thirteen Colonies. The dark red is New England, the red-brown is the Middle Colonies, and the brown is the Southern Colonies.

Agriculture was a significant economic sector, but there was also industry. Although most textiles were manufactured in Britain from raw materials imported from the colonies, textiles were produced in Pennsylvania using flax.[1] Ironworks in New York and Virginia manufactured utensils and processed pig iron for exports.

---

[1] Hurst, N. T. (2020, March 17). Made in American. Retrieved from Colonialwilliamsburg.org: https://www.colonialwilliamsburg.org/trend-tradition-magazine/spring-2018/made-american/.

Shipbuilding was an essential activity in New England, and the colonies built vessels for all kinds of use. Sloops, brigs, and frigates were readily assembled. Artisan and craft production flourished across the colonies, with skilled laborers, including blacksmiths, shoemakers, and weavers, contributing to a burgeoning local economy.

The Thirteen Colonies were less profitable than the "sugar islands." Those tiny specks of land in the Caribbean generated more wealth than all of the colonies on the Atlantic seaboard. However, business was steady, and there was a robust trade between the Thirteen Colonies and England. However, Atlantic commerce was a point of friction.

A Serious Flashpoint

External trade, especially with Europe and the Caribbean, was essential for economic prosperity, as it permitted the colonies to export their surplus goods and import necessary commodities. The Navigation Acts governed the flow of traffic to and from the Thirteen Colonies. These laws, imposed by Great Britain on its American colonies during the mid-17th and 18th centuries, were influenced by the prevailing economic concept of mercantilism, which held that national strength could be maximized through the regulation of trade.

The Navigation Acts were drafted to monopolize the trade benefits derived from British colonies. They asserted that colonial products would be exported exclusively to England or other English colonies. The Navigation Acts further stipulated that any goods sent from Europe to the colonies had to first pass through Great Britain and utilize ships crewed predominantly by English sailors. The statutes tightened British control of commerce and protected British companies from any competition from the colonies.[2]

Economically, the Navigation Acts were a problem for the colonies. They guaranteed a British market for certain colonial goods, such as tobacco and sugar. However, the laws also severely limited the colonies' ability to engage in international trade freely with countries that might have more competitive prices for goods and services. The requirement that all European goods be shipped via England increased the cost of these goods in the colonies and throttled economic growth.

[2] Wigington, P. (2018, November 29). What Were the Navigation Acts? Retrieved from Thoughtco.com: https://www.thoughtco.com/navigation-acts-4177756.

Opposition in the Colonies

Initially, some colonists accepted these trade restrictions as part of their contribution to the empire's broader economic strategy. Great Britain practiced a policy of salutary neglect in the 17th century and most of the 18th century. Salutary neglect was Britain's laissez-faire attitude about enacting laws in the colonies. In other words, the American colonists had a higher amount of freedom than other British colonies.

The Seven Years' War broke out in 1756. Conflict actually broke out in North America the year prior; that theater of the Seven Years' War is known as the French and Indian War. The war created financial hardship for Great Britain, and there was a perceived need for Parliament to tighten economic control by actively enforcing the laws that had been created. The strict enforcement of the Navigation Acts created opposition in the American colonies. The people believed the laws were creating economic constraints and saw the British monarch as an overbearing imperial ruler who exploited colonial resources without offering fair political representation or economic freedom.[3] The opposition was especially vocal in New England, where maritime trade was a cornerstone of the economy.

The Navigation Acts were more than just trade regulations. They were rules that shaped the economic landscape of the American colonies. By 1770, the effects of these acts had laid bare the contradictions between the colonies' economic aspirations and the realities of British mercantilist policy. The resentment and resistance they engendered among colonists contributed significantly to the breakdown of British colonial authority.

Enforcement led to widespread smuggling as a form of economic resistance and a political statement against the acts. The laws also fostered a political awakening among the colonists, who began questioning the legitimacy of British rule. Many began to envision an independent economic and political future.

The Source of the Problem

The Seven Years' War (1756–1763) was at the heart of the soured relations. It was a global conflict that spanned continents. Although Great Britain and her allies won, the victory was expensive.

---

[3] American History Central. (2024, February 4). The Navigation Acts. Retrieved from Americanhistorycentral.com: https://www.americanhistorycentral.com/entries/navigation-acts/.

Britain's national debt after the war was more than 130 million pounds. This debt was exacerbated by the price of maintaining and defending new territorial acquisitions. The British Parliament sought to address the financial crisis by redistributing the fiscal burdens across the empire. The American colonies, who had benefited from the successes of the British army, were expected to pay their fair share. This time, the policy of salutary neglect would not be used. Payments from the colonies were to be extracted by a series of revenue-generating laws.

Parliament enacted several legislative measures to increase revenue from the colonies and pay off the debt. A series of tax bills were passed; the most notable were the Sugar Act of 1764 and the Stamp Act of 1765. These firmly proclaimed Parliament's right to tax British overseas possessions.

The Sugar Act was not a major piece of legislation. It imposed a lower tax on sugar and molasses imports in the hopes that the tax would actually be paid (the earlier tax was mostly ignored by the colonists). The act also revised the current customs regulations to administer stricter controls on the smuggling of sugar and molasses, thereby increasing revenue and reducing obvious criminal activity. It was repealed in 1766.

The Stamp Act, however, was a more direct form of taxation. It required that a wide array of documents, newspapers, and even playing cards in the colonies be produced on stamped paper, signifying the payment of the tax. The Stamp Act imposed a cost, no matter how slight, on items that were once less expensive and, in some cases, were even free.[4]

There was a serious disconnect between the British government and the colonies. Americans were accustomed to local government and having a voice in decisions that affected them. There was no colonial representation when these taxes were imposed, so the colonists felt insulted. The Stamp Act was especially onerous and vigorously protested.

The British government's failure to anticipate the intensity of the colonies' response was a grave mistake. Parliament underestimated the colonies' political experience, which had been nurtured through decades of relative autonomy and self-governance. Some members of the British

[4] Triber, J. E. (2024, February 4). Britain Begins Taxing the Colonies: The Sugar & Stamp Acts. Retrieved from Nos.gov: https://www.nps.gov/articles/000/sugar-and-stamp-acts.htm.

Parliament recognized the risks of angering the American colonists and argued for their right to tax themselves. However, the prevailing sentiment of Parliament was that the American colonies needed to pay their fair share. These members underestimated the colonies' resolve and unity, leading to unanticipated problems.

"No taxation without representation" became a rallying cry in the colonies. The subsequent boycott of British goods and harassment of stamp distributors demonstrated the American colonists' resolve to have a voice in the policies that affected them.

The Stamp Act Congress

The opposition to the Stamp Act was so widespread that a formal response was considered necessary. A gathering of delegates from nine of the Thirteen Colonies met in New York City in October 1765 for that purpose. The final product of what would later be called the Stamp Act Congress was the adoption of the Declaration of Rights and Grievances. The Stamp Act Congress produced a bold statement that declared only the colonial legislatures had the legal authority to tax the American colonies. It was radical because this was a statement of colonial rights and the rejection of parliamentary interference in colonial matters.

Petitions were sent to King George III and Parliament demanding the repeal of the Stamp Act. The petitions stressed colonial loyalty to the British Crown and Parliament. The British government was shocked when they received the petitions, and there was pressure from British business leaders to do something to end the boycott of British products. The Stamp Act was formally repealed In February 1766. The American colonies had achieved a victory.[5]

The Stamp Act Congress was a significant event in American history. It was the first major action taken by the colonies in opposition to British policy and showed a sense of colonial unity that had not been seen before.

The Stamp Act Congress introduced several influential statesmen to colonial politics: James Otis of Massachusetts, who led the movement for the Stamp Act Congress to meet; John Dickinson of Pennsylvania, who played an essential role in drafting the petitions and other

[5] Zielinski, A. E. (2021, November 17). What Was the Stamp Act Congress and Why Did It Matter. Retrieved from Ameicanbattlefields.org: https://www.battlefields.org/learn/articles/what-was-stamp-act-congress.

documents; Stamp Act Congress chairman Timothy Ruggles of Massachusetts; and John Rutledge of South Carolina, who would later be a signatory of the United States Constitution. They would perform greater services to the American cause later.

Parliament's Dirty Little Secret

The American colonies won this battle, but the war was going to continue. On the same day the British Parliament repealed the Stamp Act, it passed the Declaratory Act. This legislation stated Parliament unequivocally had the power to bind or legislate the colonies. John Adams warned others that Parliament would use this power to attempt to tax the colonies once again.[6]

The concept of "no taxation without representation" caused controversy among members of Parliament. This argument exposed the existence of "rotten boroughs," constituencies with small electorates controlled by wealthy landowners. These boroughs allowed the landed gentry to manipulate elections in favor of their preferred candidates despite having only a handful of eligible voters. Despite their small size, rotten boroughs were able to send members of Parliament to the House of Commons.

Old Sarum, an ancient hill fort near Salisbury, was a striking example of a rotten borough. Old Sarum had no residents, yet it continued to send two members to Parliament. Meanwhile, places like Manchester that had populations numbering in the thousands had no representation in the British Parliament. The outcry from the American colonies was no doubt raising the eyebrows of those who were concerned about corruption in the British government.

In Summary

The Seven Years' War marked a significant shift in British colonial policy and set the stage for the American Revolution. The war's cost prompted Great Britain to reassess its relationship with the American colonies. Parliament responded by taxing the colonies to alleviate the national debt burden, which sparked widespread protest and resistance. The British government's inability to understand the extent of American discontent with these new laws was a crucial mistake that would be repeated again. Britain's stubborn approach to dealing with the

---

[6] Zeidan, A. (2024, February 4). Stamp Act Congress. Retrieved from Britannica.com: https://www.britannica.com/topic/Stamp-Act-Congress.

American colonies led to consequences that likely could have been avoided.

Over time, the conflict between Great Britain and its American colonies transformed into more than just a dispute over taxation. The issues of rights, representation, and national identity became prominent, highlighting the difficulties of governing an empire and the struggle to balance the need for revenue with the desire for freedom and self-governance.

The colonies faced their own economic challenges, such as income inequality and debt burden. These local issues, combined with British demands for taxes and trade restrictions, set the stage for the colonies to eventually unite in their quest for independence and the right to control their destiny.

Chapter 2: Growing Discontent

Despite the anger created by the Stamp Act, American colonists considered themselves loyal subjects of the British Crown. They just wanted a voice in how they were taxed and preferred to govern themselves with as little interference as possible. The Americans were going to be disappointed on both counts.

The years following the repeal of the Stamp Act were critical in the evolving relationship between Great Britain and the American colonies. There was increasing tension over taxation, representation, and how Great Britain would govern its extensive North American empire. Parliament enacted a series of measures intended to assert its authority over the colonies, and those legislative measures sparked strong emotions within Great Britain and America.

The Mood of the Chamber

The immediate passing of the Declaratory Act after the repeal of the Stamp Act showed Parliament's prevailing sentiment of authority and control, proclaiming Great Britain had the right and authority to legislate for the colonies "in all cases whatsoever." That was a phrase with broad meaning that could stir up trouble. Nevertheless, Parliament was determined to uphold the British government's sovereignty and ensure the colonies' financial contribution to the empire's maintenance and defense.

The members of Parliament thought that was only fair. The economic burdens of the French and Indian War had forced Great Britain to stabilize its finances, and the colonies were seen as a critical revenue source. Besides, the Thirteen Colonies had benefited from the war and were now safe from any French incursions. They should be able to help pay for the expenses incurred for protecting them.

Parliament had energetic debates regarding the appropriate response to the colonies' growing discontent and the principles at stake. The Thirteen Colonies were not without friends in the chamber.

Support for the Americans

Despite the prevailing mood of authority and control, there were members of the British Parliament who spoke up for a more nuanced approach toward the American colonies. These figures stressed the principles of liberty, the rights of Englishmen, and the dangers of escalating conflict through heavy-handed actions. They sought to prevent matters from getting worse.

Edmund Burke, a prominent Whig politician and philosopher, emerged as a vocal advocate for understanding and reconciliation with the American colonies. Burke warned about the counterproductive nature of any punitive measures, and he championed the unique character and rights of the American colonies within the empire.[7]

William Pitt, Earl of Chatham and a respected member of Parliament, supported a more conciliatory approach. Criticizing the government's policies as shortsighted, Pitt consistently called for respecting the colonies' grievances and fostering mutual respect. He believed that such empathy was not a sign of weakness. Instead, he stressed a reasonable approach to the differences that would strengthen, not diminish, the bonds of the empire.[8]

Charles James Fox, a prominent Whig parliamentarian, regularly opposed the government's disciplinary measures against the American colonies and supported the cause of American liberty. His position was grounded in a wide-ranging vision of the non-codified British constitution and the universal rights of Englishmen, which included those subjects of the Crown who resided in the colonies.[9]

[7] Oxford Learning Link. (2024, February 11). Document-Edmund Burke, Excerpts from "Conciliation with the Colonies." Retrieved from Learnnglink.oup.com: https://learninglink.oup.com/access/content/schaller-3e-dashboard-resources/document-edmund-burke-excerpts-from-conciliation-with-the-colonies-1775.
[8] Colonial Williamsburg. (2024, February 11). William Pitt's Defense of the American Colonies. Retrieved from Slaveryandrembrance.org: https://www.slaveryandremembrance.org/Almanack/life/politics/pitt.cfm.
[9] Powell, J. (1996, September 1). Charles James Fox, Valiant Voice for Liberty. Retrieved from

Collectively, these members of Parliament recognized the legitimacy of the colonies' grievances and the potential for a more harmonious resolution. Their advocacy for dialog and mutual respect displayed the complex interplay of interests and ideologies that defined the pre-revolutionary relationship between Britain and the American colonies. There were also colonial agents like Benjamin Franklin and Arthur Lee who lobbied Parliament and worked behind the scenes.

Parliamentary Obstinacy

Though there were vigorous defenses of colonial rights, most members of Parliament still wished to assert control and ensure financial contributions from the colonies to the empire's coffers. The years preceding the American Revolution were noteworthy for legislative measures that sought to reinforce parliamentary authority, often at the expense of colonial autonomy and rights.

A series of laws enacted by the British Parliament became the fulcrum around which the colonial resistance leveraged its arguments for independence. These laws, passed between 1765 and 1774, were increasingly harsh measures to raise tax revenue and impose restrictions on the American colonies.

The Laws of Parliament and the Crown

- The Declaratory Act (1766)

As mentioned above, this law affirmed Parliament's right "to bind the colonies and people of America ... in all cases whatsoever." It did not impose a tax. The Declaratory Act represented a symbolic assertion of Britain's undiminished authority over the colonies, including the right to tax them. This legislation highlighted the fundamental conflict at the heart of the colonial dispute: the question of whether Parliament had the legitimate authority to govern the colonies without their representation.

- The Townshend Acts (1767)

The Townshend Acts of 1767 introduced a new series of taxes on imports to the colonies, including glass, lead, paint, paper, and tea. Unlike the Stamp Act, which was a direct tax, the Townshend duties were indirect taxes on imports, but the distinction did little to appease the American colonists. The revenues collected were earmarked to pay the salaries of colonial governors and judges, further eroding the

Foundation for Economic Freedom: https://fee.org/articles/charles-james-fox-valiant-voice-for-liberty/.

autonomy of local colonial governments. The Townshend Acts reignited the flames of resistance, leading to boycotts of British goods and the emergence of organized protest movements.[10]

- The Tea Act (1773)

The Tea Act was an 18th-century corporate bailout. The British East India Company was running into financial trouble. The British Parliament, whose members included prominent company shareholders, passed the Tea Act in 1773, which allowed the British East India Company to sell surplus tea directly to the colonies, effectively bypassing colonial merchants and undercutting their business.

While the Tea Act actually lowered the price of tea, it reinforced the notion that the colonists were not in control of their own governance. The colonists viewed this act as a cunning attempt by Britain to make them consent to the idea of parliamentary taxation.[11]

Colonial dissent grew gradually more vocal, and the opposition became destructive with the Boston Tea Party. The British Parliament responded severely.

- The Coercive Acts (1774)

Also referred to as the Intolerable Acts, the Coercive Acts were a set of statutes intended to penalize the people of Massachusetts for the Boston Tea Party and to deter further acts of resistance. These acts closed Boston Harbor until the destroyed tea was paid for, altered the Massachusetts Charter to increase royal authority, and allowed royal bureaucrats accused of crimes in the colonies to be tried in Britain.

The passage of the Coercive Acts did not keep the colonists in line. British politicians had massively miscalculated where American sentiments lay. Rather than being cowed by disciplinary measures, the Coercive Acts unified the colonies, leading to the formation of the First Continental Congress and marking a decisive step toward independence.[12]

---

[10] History.com Editors. (2009, June 13). Townshend Acts. Retrieved from History.com: https://www.history.com/topics/american-revolution/townshend-acts.
[11] History.com Editors. (2024, February 11). British Parliament Passes Unpopular Tea Act. Retrieved from History.com: https://www.history.com/this-day-in-history/parliament-passes-the-tea-act.
[12] Mount Vernon. (2024, February 11). The Coercive (Intolerable) Acts of 1774. Retrieved from Mountvernon.org: https://www.mountvernon.org/library/digitalhistory/digital-encyclopedia/article/the-coercive-intolerable-acts-of-

Each piece of legislation chipped away at the loyalty of the American colonists to the British Crown and highlighted the untenable nature of a relationship defined by unilateral governance and economic exploitation. These acts did more than impose taxes; they challenged the identity and rights of the colonists as Englishmen.

The colonial response, characterized by intellectual arguments against taxation without representation, economic boycotts, and direct action like the Boston Tea Party, reflected a growing belief in self-governance and the inherent rights of individuals. The statutes reshaped the political landscape, fostered a sense of American identity, and sowed the seeds of a revolution that Parliament might have avoided had its members applied common sense.

The Coercive Acts and the Boston Tea Party allowed two colonial leaders to introduce themselves to the public in a big way. These men were the "influencers" of their day.

The Adams Family

It is trite to think of the American Revolution as a family affair, but one Massachusetts clan had two members who were well-known advocates of independence. Samuel (Sam) and John Adams were second cousins. Each had a different temperament, but both had a common goal.

- Sam Adams

Sam Adams stands tall in the history of the American Revolution. His name conjures up images of a firebrand orator or perhaps a shadowy figure plotting a rebellion in Boston's taverns. He was a little more complex than that, and his role in the American Revolution is fascinating.

Samuel Adams was born in Boston, Massachusetts, on September 27th, 1722. He came from a family with a solid religious backbone and possessed a puritanical sense of moral purpose that would later influence his political career. Although he began as a businessman, his growing disgust for British tax laws made him increasingly more political. Sam Adams soon became a vocal member of the Massachusetts Assembly and a well-known public figure. He was blessed with profound oratory skills and had a flair for writing influential pieces promoting colonial

---

1774/#:~:text=The%20Coercive%20Acts%20were%20meant,particular%20aspect%20of%20colo nial%20life.

rights.

Adams was at center stage in organizing opposition to the Stamp Act of 1765 and the Townshend Acts. His persuasive essays helped unite colonists from different regions, igniting conversations about self-determination.

In 1768, Adams composed the Massachusetts Circular Letter, urging colonies to resist British impositions, establishing a reputation for himself as a radical willing to challenge the current situation. He would be pivotal in organizing the Boston Tea Party in 1773 (more on that later).

Sam Adams had a knack for organizing groups for public action. He helped create the Sons of Liberty, an underground group opposed to the Crown's policies. Adams instigated various boycotts and protests. He had an unmatched ability to harness the energy of discontented colonists.[13]

- John Adams

John Adams was not as overtly passionate as his cousin, but he was just as dedicated to the cause of American independence as his hot-headed kin.

John Adams came into this world on October 30th, 1735, in Braintree (now Quincy), Massachusetts. His father was a deacon and a farmer, and he had also served in the militia. John attended Harvard and, upon graduation, began a career in law. His legal practice in Suffolk County gave him a front-row seat to the growing political friction between the colonies and Great Britain.

John Adams's erudition and gift of the written word became his most potent weapons in the prelude to the war. His abilities as an influential, persuasive writer were showcased in his political essays and responses to the tyranny perceived in British policies, such as the Stamp Act and the Townshend Acts. Essays such as "A Dissertation on the Canon and Feudal Law" (1765) passionately defended colonial rights and governance while deconstructing British arguments. These works solidified John's status as a radical voice and bolstered his credibility

[13] Boston National Historical Park. (2024, February 10). Samuel Adams: Boston's Radical Revolutionary. Retrieved from Nps.gov: https://www.nps.gov/articles/000/samuel-adams-boston-revolutionary.htm.

among colonial leaders.[14]

Both cousins would be focal points in two of the most dramatic events of the American colonies.

The Boston Massacre

To understand the events leading up to the Boston Massacre, one must consider the socioeconomic tensions that had been brewing for years. The Townshend Acts were passed into law by the British Parliament in 1767, imposing taxes on various essential goods, including paper, paint, and tea, leading to widespread protests and boycotts among colonists. The British Crown responded to these acts of defiance by deploying troops to Boston. This military occupation agitated the already resentful citizens, setting up a volatile atmosphere. The events of the Boston Massacre unfolded against the backdrop of such seething colonial anger.

On the night of March 5th, 1770, as snow blanketed the ground and tensions clouded the air, a simple dispute between a wigmaker's apprentice and a British private rapidly escalated as rowdy onlookers joined, hurling snowballs, icicles, and insults at British soldiers. The crowd continued to grow, and the British sentry called for reinforcements, which came almost immediately. The confrontation reached its climax when a soldier, hit by a club, discharged his musket, triggering a domino effect of gunfire from the other redcoats. By the time the guns went silent, three colonists lay dead, with two more dying afterward from their wounds. Blood stained the snow, and cries of anguish resounded throughout the city.

Public reaction was swift and furious. News of the bloody encounter spread like wildfire, galvanizing the already strong anti-British sentiment. Leading patriots like Samuel Adams and Paul Revere harnessed the incident's power, branding it as a "massacre" and fueling the flames of revolution through sensationalized accounts and engravings.

---

[14] Ellis, J. J. (2024, February 4). John Adams. Retrieved from Britannica.com: https://www.britannica.com/biography/John-Adams-president-of-United-States.

An engraving of the Boston Massacre by Paul Revere.
Paul Revere, CC0, via Wikimedia Commons;
https://commons.wikimedia.org/wiki/File:The_Boston_Massacre_MET_DT2086.jpg

In a time when facts were not as readily verifiable as they are today, such portrayals were the accepted narrative for many, cementing the notion of British tyranny in the hearts and minds of colonists.

The soldiers were not lynched, but they were required to stand trial. It would take considerable courage for any lawyer to defend them, but a brave man did step forward.

In Defense of Fair Justice

The British soldiers found an unlikely defender in John Adams. Although a fervent patriot, Adams believed strongly in the right to a fair trial and the rule of law.

Accepting the case posed significant risks to Adams's reputation and law practice. His potential alienation from patriotic groups, personal danger, and the suspicion of being a loyalist sympathizer meant Adams was walking a legal and social tightrope. His sense of duty to justice, however, surmounted these risks.

The crux of Adams's defense lay in proving that the soldiers acted in self-defense against a mob with violent intentions. He dissected eyewitness accounts and highlighted inconsistencies in their testimonies. Adams skillfully argued, "Facts are stubborn things; and whatever may be our wishes, our inclinations, or the dictates of our passion, they cannot alter the state of facts and evidence."

His ability to remain dispassionate, his insistence on separating fact from inflammatory fiction, and his articulation of the complexities of the law to the jury won him the case. Most of the soldiers were acquitted. The two who were proven to have fired directly into the crowd were found guilty of manslaughter and branded on the thumb as a first offense.

The acquittal of the British soldiers was a triumph for the principle of due process. Adams's successful defense highlighted his formidable skills as a lawyer and his profound belief in justice. His participation in the trial did not hamper his career; instead, it bolstered his reputation as an honest and fair man. Years later, Adams reflected on his involvement, considering it one of the best services he had rendered to America.

A painting of John Adams in 1766.
https://commons.wikimedia.org/wiki/File:John_Adams_(1766).jpg

Worthy of a Mad Hatter

The acquittal verdict did not soothe the tensions between the Thirteen Colonies and Great Britain. Other incidents occurred that highlighted the conflict between the two entities. None of them are as memorable as the Boston Tea Party.

The British government still wished to exert control and the power of taxation over its American subjects. With the Tea Act of 1773, the British government granted the struggling East India Company a monopoly over the tea trade in the colonies, effectively undercutting local merchants. It was a classic example of taxation without representation, and the act infuriated the colonists. The apparent anger of the Americans was a potent opportunity for a notorious colonial instigator named Sam Adams.[15]

Stirring the Pot

As an influential leader in the Massachusetts legislature and the clandestine Sons of Liberty, Sam Adams played a spirited role in organizing opposition to the Tea Act of 1773. Adams used his exceptional oratory skills and political network to inflame and unite the public. He guided the resistance movement that planned a bold act of defiance.

On the evening of December 16th, 1773, members of the Sons of Liberty, disguised as Mohawk Indians, boarded three British ships moored in Boston Harbor. The ships were laden with chests of tea. In a few hours, 342 chests of tea had been thrown overboard into the harbor water. The loss of this tea was significant; the Sons of Liberty destroyed around $1.7 million dollars' worth of tea in today's money.

Sam Adams was not there dumping tea into the harbor with the protestors. However, there is no doubt that he rallied the Sons of Liberty to execute such a brazen act.

Stern Consequences

As mentioned, the Boston Tea Party had immediate and momentous repercussions. In the eyes of the British government, the destruction of the tea was an unacceptable act that demanded a swift and harsh response. However, the British government's severe retaliatory measures did not force the colonists into submission. Instead, it galvanized the

---

[15] History.com Editors. (2009, October 27). Boston Tea Party. Retrieved from History.com: https://www.history.com/topics/american-revolution/boston-tea-party.

Thirteen Colonies to form a more cohesive unit of resistance to what they considered tyranny.

The clouds over the relationship between Great Britain and its American subjects were getting darker.

Chapter 3: Boston under Siege

The British Parliament was livid when the news of the Boston Tea Party reached London. A considerable fortune in tea now lay at the bottom of Boston Harbor, representing a loss for the British East India Company, investors, and the British government because of the lost tax revenue. Additionally, Parliament was angry with this display of colonial opposition to the Crown.

The members of Parliament, led by Lord North, the prime minister, sought to reaffirm the might of the British Empire and its unyielding position on colonial uprisings. The members of Parliament were ready to administer tough medicine and teach the Americans a lesson. The Coercive Acts, which were also popularly known as the Intolerable Acts in the colonies, were passed in 1774.

The Coercive Acts were a collection of statutes that aimed to assert direct control over the American colonies and punish Massachusetts for the Boston Tea Party. They included the following:

- **The Boston Port Act** effectively closed the port of Boston, paralyzing trade and crippling the economy of the colony until the destroyed tea was paid for. The British navy was tasked to blockade Boston Harbor, which started on June 1ˢᵗ, 1774. The harbor would remain closed until Boston repaid the British East India Company for the lost cargo.

- **The Massachusetts Government Act** restructured the colonial government, revoking the Massachusetts Charter of 1691. It limited town meetings and replaced the Massachusetts Council with a royally appointed one, nearly annihilating local self-governance. The act gave the royal governor authority to appoint county sheriffs and judges without the council's approval.

- **The Administration of Justice Act** permitted any royal bureaucrat who was accused of a crime to be tried in Britain or another colony instead of Massachusetts, ensuring what the colonists considered to be sham trials. The right to a fair trial by one's peers, a legal practice dating back to the Magna Carta, was eliminated.
- **The Quartering Act** required local governments to provide accommodations and supplies for British soldiers stationed in America. Soldiers were to be housed in uninhabited houses, outhouses, barns, or other buildings at the colony's expense.[16]

The mood of the British Parliament during the passage of the Coercive Acts was one of barely contained fury, wounded pride, and a firm resolve to suppress and discipline what they saw as an unruly colonial extension of the empire.

The mood of vengefulness was apparent in the acts themselves, as they were designed to punish and isolate Boston, the epicenter of colonial resistance. The laws were all punitive and showcased Parliament's readiness to penalize the colonies economically and administratively. The threat was obvious: any American colony that stood up to the Crown would endure the same treatment as Massachusetts.

Harsh Measures

The economic devastation wrought by the closing of Boston Harbor cannot be overstated. As a hub of trade and commerce, the port was the lifeblood of the local economy, and its shutdown sent ripples of hardship throughout Massachusetts. Merchants faced bankruptcy, workers met unemployment, and an entire community stared down the barrel of scarcity.

---

[16] Eisenhuth, C. (2024, February 10). The Coercive (Intolerable) Acts of 1774. Retrieved from Mountvernon.org: https://www.mountvernon.org/library/digitalhistory/digital-encyclopedia/article/the-coercive-intolerable-acts-of-1774/#:~:text=The%20Coercive%20Acts%20were%20meant,particular%20aspect%20of%20colonial%20life.

Politically, the Coercive Acts attempted to dismantle the very fabric of Massachusetts governance. The British hoped to quash the growing spirit of independence by stripping away self-determination. Instead, they forged a crucible for revolutionary fervor. Every tightening of the noose reaffirmed for many the necessity of open resistance. Socially, requiring colonial legislatures to pay for and provide accommodations for British soldiers fueled resentment and added to the growing tensions.

The British government was tired of colonial defiance and took its anger out on individuals and colonies. The most notable person who endured the British government's wrath was Benjamin Franklin.

Franklin was perhaps the most well-known American of his time. Franklin lived in London as a colonial agent for Pennsylvania (and later for Massachusetts, Georgia, and New Jersey). His role was to represent the interests of the colonies to the British government, advocating for fair treatment and liberation from oppressive legislation. Regrettably, this distinguished man was caught up in the conflict and was singled out for abuse before the King's Privy Council.

The humiliation stemmed from a stack of letters. Franklin had obtained a pile of correspondence written by Thomas Hutchinson, who was the royal governor of Massachusetts, and other officials, which he then sent back to America. These letters called for an abridgment of the rights and freedoms of the colonists, suggesting they were too liberty-minded. When the letters were eventually leaked and published by the *Boston Gazette*, they caused an uproar amongst the colonists since they were seen as a direct threat to their liberties. Hutchinson and his supporters were outraged and demanded retribution. The Crown was only too happy to oblige.

On January 29th, 1774, Franklin was called before the Privy Council in the Whitehall Palace's "Cockpit" to address the leak of the letters. He stood to defend his actions but was instead subjected to harsh public censuring. Solicitor General Alexander Wedderburn unleashed a torrent of verbal abuse upon Franklin, attacking his character and reputation. Franklin was accused of being a thief and a spy and portrayed as embodying the colonies' ingratitude.

In a hall filled with spectators, Franklin was humiliated and ridiculed without the opportunity for a proper defense. He stood in stoic silence, absorbing the mockery and jeers, powerless against the assaults of Wedderburn's words. Franklin would later compare the episode to bull-baiting. The man was thoroughly disgraced.[17]

Franklin's feelings after the Privy Council meeting are best summarized in a letter he wrote but did not send to William Strahan, an English printer and publisher:

"You are a Member of Parliament, and one of that Majority which has doomed my Country to Destruction. You have begun to burn our Towns, and murder our People. Look upon your hands! They are stained with the Blood of your Relations! You and I were long Friends; You are now my Enemy, and I am, Yours."[18]

The incident was pivotal in changing Franklin's view of the British Empire and its leaders. He had once worked tirelessly for reconciliation between America and Britain, but by the time he returned home, he had become disenchanted and aligned with those advocating for complete independence. Benjamin Franklin would soon prove how potent an enemy he was.

Colonial Defiance in the Face of Adversity

Despite these challenges, Boston's response was emblematic of the times. Far from breaking under pressure, the city became a beacon of rebellion. Massachusetts, the focal point of British punishment, quickly became a hub for colonial defiance.

The patriots in Massachusetts coordinated a series of underground meetings, which culminated in the formation of shadow governments known as Provincial Congresses. These groups, authorized by the people, met in secret and began taking over the functions of local governance.

Support for Massachusetts resonated throughout the other colonies. In what became known as the Suffolk Resolves, the colonies were urged not to obey the Intolerable Acts, and the residents of Massachusetts were asked to appoint militia officers and arm themselves. The Suffolk Resolves also called for economic sanctions against Great Britain.[19]

---

[17] Founders Online. (2024, February 10). The Final Hearing. Retrieved from Founders Online: https://founders.archives.gov/documents/Franklin/01-21-02-0018.
[18] Franklin, Benjamin. (2024, February 10). Benjamin Franklin in His Own Words. Retrieved from Loc.gov: https://www.loc.gov/exhibits/franklin/franklin-break.html.
[19] American History Central. (2024, February 10). The Suffolk Resolves. Americanhistorycentral.com. Retrieved from Suffolk Resolves Summary 1774: https://www.americanhistorycentral.com/entries/suffolk-resolves/.

Colonies rallied to this common cause. Virginia's House of Burgesses declared a "Day of Fasting and Prayer," showing solidarity with Massachusetts and challenging the legitimacy of the British Parliament. South Carolina created a Committee of Correspondence, which facilitated communication and coordination among the colonies, creating a united front against British influence. Eleven colonies would eventually have their own committees.

Public demonstrations were held in New York and Pennsylvania to educate the local populations about the unjust nature of the Intolerable Acts and their implications for colonial liberty. A network of committees, the rise of the Provincial Congresses, and the support expressed through aid to Boston all provided evidence that the colonists would not buckle under the weight of oppressive legislation.

The response to the Intolerable Acts demonstrated a level of political maturity and unity that had not been seen before in the colonies. These collective acts of defiance and the resultant convening of the First Continental Congress provided the organizational framework necessary to mount a successful challenge to British rule.

Parliament's refusal to see reason was a tremendous opportunity for colonial radicals and rabble-rousers. The Coercive Acts were an inspiration for these 18th-century influencers. Samuel Adams made sure to take advantage. He was a very busy man in 1774.

Sam Adams worked tirelessly to promote the Suffolk Resolves, which called for outright resistance to the Intolerable Acts, rejecting their legitimacy and asserting colonial rights. His ability to navigate and negotiate with other delegates led to the endorsement of the Suffolk Resolves by the First Continental Congress.[20]

The Meeting of a Congress

The embers of unrest found their flames fanned by the Intolerable Acts. These laws would be the catalyst for the First Continental Congress. Adams knew then that the time for talk was nearing its end and that the time for unified action was upon them.

In an atmosphere of escalating tensions, the First Continental Congress was convened on September 5th, 1774, in Carpenters' Hall in

---

[20] Boston National Historical Park. (2024, February 10). Samuel Adams: Boston's Radical Revolutionary. Retrieved from Nps.gov: https://www.nps.gov/articles/000/samuel-adams-boston-revolutionary.htm.

Philadelphia. The assembly was born from a collective colonial need to address grievances against the British Crown and to form a unified front. The Congress brought together representatives from twelve of the thirteen colonies, with Georgia being the exception.[21]

The First Continental Congress laid the groundwork for American unity in the face of British oppression. It displayed intercolonial cooperation and political solidarity. It was hoped that a strong message to the royal government would prevent further infringements on what the American colonists perceived were their rights.

Carpenters' Hall in Philadelphia.
https://commons.wikimedia.org/wiki/File:CarpentersHall00.jpg

[21] Horan, Katherine. (2024, February 10). First Continental Congress. Retrieved from Mountvernon.org: https://www.mountvernon.org/library/digitalhistory/digital-encyclopedia/article/first-continental-congress/#:~:text=One%20of%20the%20Congress%27s%20first,and%20to%20raise%20a%20militia.

The Leaders

Those who attended were not drawn from the common folk, but the leadership was still diverse. There were wealthy landowners, lawyers, and merchants, each of whom promoted their colony's wants and needs. Principal assembly members included Samuel Adams and John Adams from Massachusetts, John Jay from New York, and George Washington from Virginia.

Sam Adams understood the cultural significance of the First Continental Congress. It was not merely a gathering of representatives; it was also the embodiment of an American identity separate and distinct from the British. His push for unity and his argument that the fight against the Crown was everyone's fight helped forge a nationalistic spirit that transcended boundaries.

In essence, Sam Adams did more than shape opinions about the Continental Congress; he used it as a platform to bind the colonies together for a shared purpose, creating momentum for independence.

John Adams entered the First Continental Congress, aware of the colony's burgeoning civil unrest. Fueled by his fiery commitment to colonial rights and legal acumen, Adams became a central figure in advocating for resistance against onerous British policies.

Adams tackled the complex legal and philosophical underpinnings of colonial rights. His talent for persuasion and tireless work ethic helped to draft resolutions that underscored the legitimacy of the Congress's cause. Adams strived to bridge provincial conflicts that threatened unity, understanding that a collective front was the only viable path against British dominion.

John Jay was less famous than other attendees, but he quickly distinguished himself through his pragmatic approach to diplomacy. A conservative by nature, Jay was not an immediate advocate for outright rebellion; instead, he favored moderate policies and strategic discourse with the Crown.

Jay's meticulous nature shone through in his role during the Congress. He contributed to the drafting of the "Address to the People of Great Britain," in which he articulated the colonists' grievances and desires in a firm yet conciliatory manner, reflecting his foresight and desire for a peaceful resolution.

George Washington brought his stately presence and a sense of steadfastness and resolve to the First Continental Congress. His military experience and leadership during the French and Indian War gave him a reputation of unwavering dedication to the colonial cause.

While Washington was not as vocal as some of his colleagues, his contributions came through his composure and the respect he commanded from fellow delegates. His presence alone was a testament to the seriousness of the First Continental Congress's intent, and when he spoke, it was with the clarity and conviction of a leader fully aware of the gravity of their situation.

Many other men attended the Congress, and most showcased facets of leadership, be it through enthusiastic advocacy, strategic negotiation, or stoic unity, inspiring others to take action.

The Debate and the Results

Since the delegates came from different colonies, they had varied attitudes toward rebellion. Some sought reconciliation with Great Britain, while others, like Samuel Adams, believed independence was the only viable path forward. The delegates debated passionately. By the time the First Continental Congress adjourned, several resolutions and recommendations had been determined.

The First Continental Congress endorsed the Suffolk Resolves, which rejected the Massachusetts Government Act. Instead, they would prepare for armed resistance against the British. The Congress created a Declaration of Rights and Grievances, establishing the colonies' entitlement to participation in government as extensions of the Crown and cataloging the perceived infringements and abuses by Britain. This asserted a political identity separate from Great Britain despite still claiming allegiance to the British Crown.

The most significant outcome was the Continental Association. It set forth a system of non-importation, non-exportation, and non-consumption to boycott British goods. This economic weapon aimed to pressure Britain into repealing burdensome legislation.

A thread of loyalty to the Crown persisted in the First Continental Congress. The delegates chiefly sought to address specific injustices rather than pursue outright separation. However, as events unfolded, the people's alignment with Britain slowly disintegrated.

Parliament's Reaction

The First Continental Congress was a gathering that signaled the colonial resolve against what they saw as oppressive British policies. But what was the reaction across the ocean. How did politicians respond within the hallowed halls of the British Parliament?

Parliament's reaction was mixed and highlighted vast differences in opinion between members. Some foresaw the danger of escalation and advocated for reconciliation. Others, however, interpreted the Congress's actions as outright defiance, warranting a firm response to maintain British authority. The dominating sentiment was that concessions would only encourage the rebellious spirit.

The debates within Parliament were tense and fraught with emotion, reflecting the gravity of the situation. There were those, such as Lord North, who felt the colonies' actions could not go unchecked. Others, like Edmund Burke and William Pitt the Elder, argued the American colonists were entitled to certain rights as Englishmen and that Parliament should aim to mend the relationship, not deepen the chasm. In various speeches and proposals, they urged their peers to recognize the legitimate concerns of the colonies stemming from legislation like the Stamp Act and the Tea Act.

The colonies represented significant commercial interests, and their cooperation was essential for the mercantile system's smooth functioning. Despite this, Parliament chose to prioritize asserting authority over securing these economic ties. The opposition argued the principle of parliamentary sovereignty was at stake. To many British lawmakers, conceding to colonial demands would be tantamount to admitting that Parliament did not hold ultimate legislative authority over the colonies. Conceding to the North American colonies might mean conceding to the colonists living on the profitable Caribbean islands.

Ultimately, the Crown viewed the First Continental Congress as an illegal assembly and rendered any of its decisions null.

At the heart of Parliament's reaction was a fundamental misunderstanding: the British saw the First Continental Congress as a challenge to their authority rather than a response to policies that the colonists considered unjust. The reaction of the British Parliament stemmed from the inherent conflict between the need to control a vast empire and the growing desire of the colonies for self-determination.

<u>In Summary</u>

The First Continental Congress was a precursor to the Declaration of Independence and the eventual American Revolutionary War. Its legacy is enshrined not just in the outcomes and correspondence that originated from it but also in the unity and resolve it fostered among diverse colonies that had different interests and cultures. At the time, however, the changes the First Continental Congress hoped for did not happen. Parliament underestimated the colonists' resolve, leading to a hardened stance that aggravated tensions. The British response served only to alienate the colonies further, paving the way for actions with drastic consequences.

There was a mutual disagreement that no longer permitted calm debate or reasonable resolution. Both sides were moving toward a point where bullets were more appealing than words. The final decision about the future would not happen in London or Philadelphia; it would be made on the village green of two small towns.

Chapter 4: The Shot

The year 1775 was a pivotal one for the Thirteen Colonies. A series of cultural, economic, political, and social events stirred the pot of revolution, leading to the fateful encounters in Lexington and Concord.

These events did not occur in isolation; instead, they culminated in rising tensions and grievances that had been festering for years. Parliament's reaction to the First Continental Congress shattered attempts at reasonable reconciliation with Great Britain.

Amidst the backdrop of legislative acts was the silent, steadfast preparation for conflict. The Minutemen—colonial part-time militiamen—began drilling more frequently. Gunpowder and arms were stockpiled, and colonial leaders, including Samuel Adams and John Hancock, roused support through the Committees of Correspondence. Some Americans hoped for a peaceful resolution, but many were less sanguine. Patrick Henry appeared to sum up the popular mood when he said, "The war is inevitable—and let it come! I repeat it, sir, let it come."[22] People were starting to prepare for war.

The Power of Communication

Communication in the face of oppression took a formalized shape through the Committees of Correspondence. This system was the Facebook of its time—a revolutionary fiber-optic network minus the

---

[22] Wirt, William (ed. 1973). Give Me Liberty or Give Me Death. Retrieved from Colonial Williamsburg: https://www.colonialwilliamsburg.org/learn/deep-dives/give-me-liberty-or-give-me-death/.

optics and fibers. These committees served as the information highways among the Thirteen Colonies, spreading news, coordinating responses to British policies, and sowing the seeds of unity for colonial resistance.

By 1775, the Committees of Correspondence had evolved into powerful tools of diplomacy and advocacy. They did not stand still; instead, they morphed into dynamic bodies advocating resistance and alignment against the overreach of imperial governance. These committees worked tirelessly to coordinate stances regarding British policies, nurtured intercolonial partnerships, and rallied support for the burgeoning cause of independence.

These instruments of colonial communication excelled in a few pivotal roles:

- Dissemination of information: Acting like a colonial "pony express," these committees rapidly spread the news of British actions along with interpretations that boosted the patriotic cause.

- Unity: The committees fortified a sense of solidarity and collective resolve among the colonists, encouraging shared ideals and goals.

- Local leadership: Serving as local and intercolonial governing bodies, the committees heavily influenced colonial policies and local governance.

- Event chronicling: They meticulously documented events and British policy outcomes, creating a written record that served as potent propaganda and historical documentation.

The committees' incessant efforts empowered individuals, instilled a collective consciousness among the American people, and ignited the flame of self-determination. They kept the fires of resistance burning brightly.[23]

Radicals kept colonists alert to what was happening and stirred public opinion. Understanding who the radicals were in the months leading up to the American Revolution in 1775 is crucial. These weren't mindless rebels without a cause; they were strategic, driven, and embraced revolutionary sentiments that would realign the trajectory of an entire

---

[23] Longley, R. (2020, October 14). Committees of Correspondence: Definition and History. Retrieved from Thoughtco.com: https://www.thoughtco.com/committees-of-correspondence-definition-and-history-5082089.

nation.

These leaders did not work in isolation; they spearheaded a network of like-minded revolutionaries, navigating through British constraints to orchestrate a full-scale movement toward revolution. They weren't necessarily middle-class businessmen. Among these firebrands was one man who happened to be one of the wealthiest men in the colonies.

John Hancock: Plutocrat and Patriot

In the story of the American Revolution, John Hancock is a man whose name has become synonymous with bold signatures, but his deeds reached far beyond the flourish of a quill. The year 1775 found John Hancock at the epicenter of colonial resistance. His financial support and leadership through various colonial committees marked him as a target for British authorities. His proximity to pivotal figures like Samuel Adams and Paul Revere linked him irrevocably to the cause for American independence.

Born on January 23rd, 1737, in Braintree, Massachusetts, Hancock inherited a substantial fortune from his uncle, Thomas Hancock, which granted him both affluence and influence in the Massachusetts colony. As a merchant, Hancock's involvement in trade introduced him to the harsh realities of British colonial policies and the simmering discontent of the colonies. Given his considerable wealth, he ought to have been a loyalist, but he was not.

He sympathized with the radicals, and he might have been one of those behind the scenes who organized the Boson Tea Party. The British suspected him of being a smuggler, but John Adams was able to help Hancock escape being convicted of smuggling charges.[24]

John Hancock's statute rose when he was elected president of the Second Continental Congress in 1775. This significant role placed him at the helm of colonial affairs during critical moments. Hancock bore the responsibility of uniting disparate colonies, galvanizing military efforts, and facilitating the dialog that would eventually draft the Declaration of Independence.

The British Commander

In the history of the American Revolution, few British figures are as simultaneously prominent and controversial as Lieutenant General

---

[24] NCC Staff. (2021, May 24). 10 Fascinating Facts About John Hancock. Retrieved from Constitutioncenter.org: https://constitutioncenter.org/blog/10-fascinating-facts-about-john-hancock

Thomas Gage. He played a pivotal role as a British commander during the early stages of the American Revolution. Gage served as the governor of Massachusetts Bay and the commander in chief of the British forces in North America. His tenure in this volatile environment was marked by increasing tensions between the American colonies and the British Crown.

Thomas Gage's relationship with North America was long-standing. He first arrived on the continent as a lieutenant colonel in 1754 to partake in the French and Indian War. After various military appointments and a brief return to England, Gage came back to the colonies in 1763 as the commander of all British forces in North America. His profound familiarity with the land and its people spanned over two decades.

During his years on the continent, Gage had the opportunity to develop his opinions about the American colonies and their inhabitants. These perceptions would influence his strategies and policies in the years leading up to the revolution.

Gage's responsibilities were extensive and multifaceted. As the military governor, he was tasked with implementing and enforcing the increasingly unpopular acts passed by the British Parliament. His duties included maintaining order, overseeing the colonial administration, and commanding the British troops stationed across North America. He was the linchpin in Britain's efforts to sustain colonial obedience, an unenviable position amid the rising tide of revolutionary spirit.

Thomas Gage.
John Singleton Copley, CC0, via Wikimedia Commons;
https://commons.wikimedia.org/wiki/File:Thomas_Gage_John_Singleton_Copley.jpeg

While Gage recognized the resourcefulness and resolve of the colonists, which he gleaned from their performance in past conflicts, he also harbored a certain disdain for their rebellious streak. In correspondence with his superiors, Gage frequently expressed a belief that American agitators were a minority, though a loud one, and that many colonists remained loyal to the Crown.

However, as the agitation grew and the whisper of revolution became a clamor, Gage faced mounting challenges. His attempts to constrain the patriots, such as the enforcement of the Coercive Acts and his actions leading up to the Battles of Lexington and Concord, reveal a man who underestimated the resolve and capabilities of a populace inching closer to war.

Gage's stance on the rebels hardened over time. With reports of undisciplined colonial militias and the chaos of mob actions, Gage's dispatches to London became increasingly critical of the American colonies. Under pressure, he advocated for more troops and stricter measures, which only fanned the flames of rebellion.

Training in Secret: Colonial Militias

On the cusp of revolutionary outbreak, militias were quintessential to the defensive and, at times, offensive strategies of the colonies. While British soldiers were stationed in Boston, militias were rallied throughout the rural regions of Massachusetts and beyond. The militias were composed of local men, from farmers to tradespeople, ready to defend their rights and homes. They trained persistently, their drills shrouded in secrecy to avoid punitive actions by the British.

It was within this crucible of unrest that the militia system began to transform. Leaders like Samuel Adams and John Hancock in Massachusetts, amongst other colonial firebrands, started to view these local forces as defenders and instruments of potential insurrection.

Militias engaged in secret assemblies and drills. These were not the regular, somewhat leisurely musterings that characterized peacetime training. They were intense and frequent and were held under the guise of normalcy. By day, the militia members were tradesmen, farmers, and artisans; by evening, they were soldiers in training.

Books, such as *A Plan of Discipline, Composed for the Use of the Militia of the County of Norfolk*, penned by William Windham and George Townshend in 1759, found their way across the Atlantic, providing a framework for military exercises. Inspired by such manuals, the militias were drilled with a newfound sense of urgency, learning to maneuver, fire, reload, and respond to commands efficiently. The colonists had one strategy that came from personal experience for many. They had fought the Native Americans throughout the years and learned the value of ambush and the use of the woods for defense.

Understanding the necessity of being well equipped for an impending conflict, militias began stockpiling weapons and gunpowder. This was no simple task under the watchful eyes of British officials.

Each community had committees of safety, which played a pivotal role in the collection and distribution of arms and munitions. For instance, in Salem and Marblehead, Massachusetts, secret stashes of gunpowder were amassed, which would later become vital to the cause. All these preparations suggest that the British army would not be facing a mob but groups of colonists who had an idea of how to wage war.

The Days Before

An encounter that heavily foreshadowed the Battles of Lexington and Concord was the Lexington Powder Alarm in September 1774. British troops moved to seize colonial gunpowder, leading to widespread alarm and the formation of militia units. Though this event ended without bloodshed, it served as a rehearsal for the battles to come.[25]

Communication between colonies was essential, and a clandestine network of spies and messengers was established to share intelligence about British troop movements and garrison strengths. The famous "Midnight Ride" of Paul Revere was only one of many critical information relay operations enacted during the months leading up to the clashes in April 1775.

In the weeks leading up to April 19th, 1775, the tension between the British troops in Boston and the Massachusetts colonists was palpable. General Gage was acutely aware of the restive mood of rebellion. He had orders to disarm the rebels and arrest their leaders.

Yet, the colonial militia, or Minutemen, were ominous shadows sliding through the towns and countryside, readying muskets and munitions. Intelligence of such activities was well known to Gage, who had dispatched spies throughout the region. In response, he planned a

---

[25] Rust, R. (2023, April 14). The Powder Alarm of Massachusetts in 1774. Retrieved from Americanhistorycentral.com: https://www.americanhistorycentral.com/entries/powder-alarm-1774-massachusetts/.

tactical strike designed to seize colonial arms stored at Concord and to capture revolutionary leaders like John Hancock and Samuel Adams, who were rumored to be staying near Lexington.

On the other side were the colonial leaders. Foreseeing conflict, they strategically spread out their stockpiles of weapons and ammunition across various rural locations. The atmosphere was one of silent resolve; conversations were held in hushed tones as plans were meticulously laid out for the anticipated call to arms.

The colonial leaders also established intricate networks of messengers and signals to alert the countryside of any British advances. The night before the skirmishes at Lexington and Concord, Gage sent seven hundred troops to destroy the colonials' weapons cache. Paul Revere and William Dawes embarked on their famous midnight ride to warn Adams and Hancock and rouse the Minutemen.

<u>The Midnight Ride</u>

"LISTEN, my children, and you shall hear

Of the midnight ride of Paul Revere,

On April 18, in Seventy-five;

Hardly a man is now alive

Who remembers that famous day and year."

People are thrilled by the cadence of that famous poem by Henry Wadsworth Longfellow. It is exciting to read and fun to imagine that ride through the night to warn people of the British march. Longfellow told a great story, but he used considerable poetic license. What happened that evening was quite different from what he wrote.

The ride was not spontaneous; it was a carefully coordinated alarm through lantern signals and a relay of riders. Paul Revere, along with William Dawes and later joined by Dr. Samuel Prescott, raced against time to warn communities and urge Hancock and Adams to go into hiding. Revere was captured before reaching Concord, and it was Prescott who successfully carried the news to the men. Because of Henry Wadsworth Longfellow's famous poem, Revere's role is fixed in the American spirit as the herald of revolution.[26]

---

[26] The Paul Revere House. (2024, February 14). The Real Story of Paul Revere's Ride. Retrieved from Paulreverehouse.org: https://www.paulreverehouse.org/the-real-story/.

Battles Fought

Just before dawn on April 19th, 1775, the militias were called upon to challenge the British march toward Concord. Those months of secretive preparations had paid dividends. As dawn approached on that fateful April day, British forces under Lieutenant Colonel Francis Smith and Major John Pitcairn arrived in Lexington. They encountered a ragtag band of American militiamen, led by Captain John Parker, lined upon the common. Confusion ensued, a shot rang out—the legendary "shot heard round the world"—and eight colonists lay dead in the aftermath. Historians still debate who fired the first shot, but its impact was nevertheless unmistakable.

The British column then moved to Concord, where they were stymied by the absence of most of the munitions they had come to destroy, cleverly hidden by the foresighted colonists. As they searched the town, colonial reinforcements swelled, leading to a confrontation at Concord's North Bridge. A more organized battle ensued, and the British were forced to retreat.

The retreat damaged the British column. The colonists used a strategy they learned long ago from the Native Americans. The Minutemen did not openly confront their red-coated adversary; they picked away at the retreating British by firing from behind trees or underbrush and then vanishing into the landscape before the British could respond. As the British neared Boston, their ranks were thinned, exhaustion had set in, and morale had plummeted.

By the time the column reached the safety of Boston, the British had suffered 19 officers and 250 regulars killed or wounded. American casualties were less than one hundred. The Americans considered this a strategic victory that proved they could stand up against one of the world's most powerful armies.[27]

The Aftermath of the Fight

The Battles of Concord and Lexington were not isolated events but rather the result of a complex interplay between sociopolitical movements and stealthy military preparations. These confrontations set the stage for a war that would challenge the might of the British Empire

---

[27] BritishBattles.com. (2024, February 14). Battle of Lexington and Concord. Retrieved from BritishBattles.com: https://www.britishbattles.com/war-of-the-revolution-1775-to-1783/battle-of-lexington-and-concord/.

and raise the banner of independence for the nascent United States of America.

What happened that April morning was more than a mere military engagement; symbolically, it marked the decisive step from peaceful protest to armed resistance in the colonies. Ralph Waldo Emerson later termed the conflict at North Bridge as "the shot heard round the world," encapsulating the global significance of America's fight for independence.

The ripples of Lexington and Concord expanded far beyond Massachusetts. The colonies quickly became a hive of revolutionary activity. The First Continental Congress had adjourned with the understanding that another one could be called for in the future if things did not improve. Given the events at Lexington and Concord, the Second Continental Congress was assembled on May 10th, 1775, at Independence Hall in Philadelphia.

A Revolutionary Congress

The delegates gathered at this second historic Continental Congress represented a cross-section of the revolution's leaders. There was John Adams, who pushed for independence from the outset, and there were moderate figures like John Dickinson who sought reconciliation with the Crown. These men played a significant role in defining the American cause and shaping the revolution's trajectory.

On June 14th, 1775, the Second Continental Congress voted to create a Continental Army from the militia units gathered outside Boston. The Congress went further and drafted a statement explaining the colonies' reasons for taking up arms. The Declaration of the Causes and Necessity of Taking Up Arms, issued on July 6th, 1775, outlined the grievances the colonies had with the British government and their commitment to defending their rights and liberties. The Second Continental Congress was not yet ready to declare full separation from the British Crown, though. The Olive Branch Petition, an attempt at securing peace with the Crown, was signed by the delegates on July 8th.

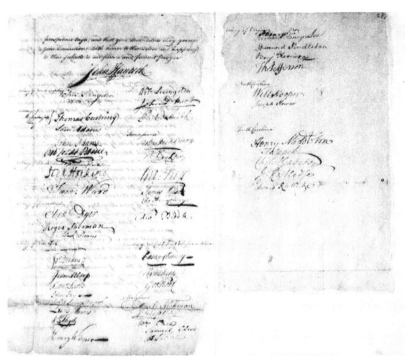

The Olive Branch Petition. You can see John Hancock's signature at the top of the left page

In Summary

The years of debate and attempts to find some means of compromise were over. The efforts to persuade the British Crown that there were alternatives for addressing colonial concerns and that colonial representation in Parliament was necessary failed. The Second Continental Congress's resolutions proved that words were no longer sufficient.

The British Parliament bears responsibility for what happened in the spring and summer of 1775. If its members had listened to Burke and other colonial sympathizers, there might have been a way to raise the needed money without harsh measures. Unfortunately, Parliament was obstinate and fixed in its resolve to be the only judge of what needed to be done. What happened next would be eight years of war that pitted the greatest army and navy of Europe against thirteen colonies whose armed forces were primarily composed of civilians.

Chapter 5: Early Successes

At the dawn of war, George Washington was a leader weighed down by the enormity of the task before him. Appointed as the commander in chief of what would become the Continental Army on June 15th, 1775, his mantle was one of responsibility and expectation. He is a fascinating study in leadership. He possessed a stoic, unyielding presence that inspired confidence and loyalty.

Portrait of George Washington.
https://en.wikipedia.org/wiki/File:Gilbert_Stuart_Williamstown_Portrait_of_George_Washington.jpg

Washington was faced with a confluence of challenges. The Continental Army was in its infancy and comprised a disparate collection of militias. More organized training, equipment, and, crucially, experience in fighting as a unified force were needed. Succeeding in battles was critical to establishing the legitimacy of the American cause and persuading wavering colonists to support the rebellion.

Creating a Military Force

Washington's primary objective was to transform the ragtag colonial forces into a disciplined army capable of confronting the professional British military.

In the early stages of the war, the Continental Army was an unorganized and untrained mix of volunteers lacking discipline and experience. Washington recognized the need for a complete overhaul to turn these civilians into effective fighters. The first step was establishing a regular army distinct from the state militias. The Continentals could operate as a unified force rather than disparate state units by unifying command and streamlining logistics.[28]

Under Washington's guidance, uniformity in discipline and dress became required. Each day, troops participated in military drills that were focused on mastering essential maneuvers. By drilling the concepts of formation, movement, and firepower, Washington instilled a sense of order and control that was essential in battle. Moreover, implementing a standard uniform and regulations for wear cultivated a sense of unity and belonging among soldiers, inspiring collective identity and purpose.[29]

Training was paramount. Soldiers needed to learn not just how to march in formation but also how to load and fire their weapons efficiently, maneuver on the battlefield, and, most importantly, withstand the rigors of war. Regular training exercises and mock battles simulated real-world conditions, honing the skills of the troops and preparing them for actual combat.

Morale was both the fuel and the result of these undertakings. Promotions were based on merit rather than birth, instilling a sense of a meritocracy that could inspire ambition among the enlisted men and

[28] William P. Kladky, P. (2024, February 15). Continental Army. Retrieved from Mountvernon.org: https://www.mountvernon.org/library/digitalhistory/digital-encyclopedia/article/continental-army/.
[29] Battlefields.org. (2024, January 23). 10 Facts: The Continental Army. Retrieved from Battlefields.org: https://www.battlefields.org/learn/articles/10-facts-continental-army.

promote loyalty to their superiors.

Beyond that, Washington also recognized the significance of non-combat skills. Camp followers, responsible for cooking, cleaning, and other support roles, were integral to maintaining the army. These civilians, often women and children, contributed to the communal spirit and practical functioning of the military, playing a silent but influential role in the war effort.

The transformation of the Continental Army from civilians to soldiers is a saga replete with heroism and sacrifice, but it is also one that illustrates the vital importance of cohesive leadership, strategic foresight, and dedicated preparation.

The Trials of Thomas Gage

On the British side stood General Thomas Gage, who was caught in a conundrum with no easy solution. The British commander was required to face challenges, make decisions, and direct strategies that would determine the direction of the British Empire in North America.

Gage was not facing a small band of discontents. The American colonists were no ordinary insurgents; they were spirited, intimately familiar with the terrain, and motivated by a just, if not desperate, cause. The challenges they presented to Gage were manifold. How does one quell a rebellion amongst one's own, especially when the lines of loyalty are so blurred? Gage had to wrestle with preconceived notions of colonial obedience and British superiority that now seemed obsolete in the face of American resolve. The military force Gage had at his disposal was sufficient to garrison British territory but hardly enough to deal with a revolt that stretched down the Atlantic seaboard. His Boston garrison was no match for a fledgling revolution that was spreading.

The colonists were arming themselves, but where were their depots, and how many men did the colonies? These were more than military questions; they were also political questions that had serious consequences. Failure to act upon gathered intelligence or, worse, engage in a mistaken action that would be deemed overly aggressive by local populations could lead to a damning loss of trust and fidelity. On the other hand, underestimating the colonists' firepower could have equally dire consequences for Gage's own forces.

General Gage also faced a logistical nightmare. The American colonies covered huge areas. Maintaining and sustaining an orderly campaign in the vast expanses of America was almost impossible.

Supplies, reinforcements, and communication lines would be long and vulnerable.

The harshness of winter, disease, and the fierce independence of the American colonies were going to be constant adversaries. Gage's decisions had to weigh strategic value against the very tangible limitations of space and means.

The immediate problem for the British commander was Boston and the appearance of a hostile force on the outskirts of town. Gage received 4,500 reinforcements under the command of Major General William Howe in June 1775. He would have to endure a siege or attempt a breakout.[30]

The Siege of Boston

An initial objective of the Continental Army was to take Boston back from the British. Taking Boston would serve to secure the New England region, which was a hotbed of revolutionary fervor. Thousands of colonial militiamen encamped on the outskirts of the city. The hills surrounding Boston provided an advantageous position from which artillery could command the town and harbor below.

Recognizing this, colonial leaders appointed a commander to oversee the siege of Boston. General Artemas Ward was a respected militia officer with experience in the French and Indian War. He was placed in command. One of his officers, Colonel William Prescott, led some of the soldiers onto the peninsula and built an earthen redoubt on Breed's Hill.

The fortifications constructed on that elevation worried General Gage because it tightened the colonial siege of Boston. He decided that a show of force might break the siege and show British military superiority.

On June 17th, 1775, Gage ordered an assault. Approximately 2,300 British regulars under William Howe's command attacked the redoubt. Although popular legend calls this engagement the Battle of Bunker Hill, most of the actual fighting took place on Breed's Hill.

The battle's outset was marked by the colonists' determination and British underestimation of their opponent. As the British advanced, the famous command attributed to a colonial officer rang out: "Don't fire until you see the whites of their eyes!" This directive aimed to maximize

---

[30] Hickman, K. (2019, June 13). American Revolution: General Thomas Gage. Retrieved from Thoughtco.com: https://www.thoughtco.com/general-thomas-gage-2360620.

the impact of the limited ammunition available to the colonial militia. It required three attempts, but the British eventually captured the hill.[31]

However, it was a Pyrrhic victory. The British suffered more than one thousand dead or wounded in taking Breed's Hill, including many officers. Furthermore, it was a morale booster for the colonists. The battle revealed the firm resolve of the colonial forces and demonstrated that untrained American militias could stand up to British regulars in battle. The heavy losses sustained by the British army also served as a notice to Great Britain that suppressing the rebellion would only come with significant cost.

General Gage was finished. He was recalled home in October, and Howe was placed in temporary command. There was a change of command on the colonial side as well, as George Washington arrived to take over the siege operations.

Washington aimed to establish a network of fortifications around Boston. This would not only serve as a defensive perimeter but also as a training ground for the Continental Army. Fortifying the city was an opportunity to educate his troops in the arts of war while simultaneously containing the British forces in a strategic stalemate.

Washington was faced with a significant challenge. The Continental Army surrounding Boston was low on ammunition and artillery. Washington needed both to conclude the siege successfully. He got what he needed thanks to a ragtag group of Vermont militiamen.

The Taking of Fort Ticonderoga

Fort Ticonderoga was situated on the shores of Lake Champlain in upstate New York and served as a cornerstone in the strategic waterway connecting Canada to the Hudson River Valley. Originally named Fort Carillon by the French, who constructed it in 1755, it was designed as a bulwark against British forces during the French and Indian War. In 1775, the British were using the fort as a central munitions depot. As tensions between the American colonies and the British Crown escalated, Fort Ticonderoga became vitally important due to its large artillery stores. Capturing the fort would give Washinton what he desperately needed.

---

[31] American Battlefield Trust. (2024, February 15). Bunker Hill. Retrieved from Battlefields.org: https://www.battlefields.org/learn/revolutionary-war/battles/bunker-hill.

Only fifty soldiers guarded the fort. A large force was not necessary, but the attackers had to be familiar with the territory and able to approach the fortification undetected. The assault fell to the Green Mountain Boys, who lived in the area.

The Green Mountain Boys were a group of amateur soldiers from the present-day state of Vermont, then known as the New Hampshire Grants (land grants given by New Hampshire). Led by the charismatic Ethan Allen, the Green Mountain Boys were fighting to maintain control of their lands against New York settlers. When the opportunity arose to join the American Revolution, their motivations became aligned with the broader colonial cause. Their expedition included a controversial figure of the American Revolution.

Benedict Arnold was, at the time, an ambitious officer. Arnold was appointed a colonel by the Massachusetts Committee of Safety and assigned the task of seizing Fort Ticonderoga. Upon learning of the Green Mountain Boys' similar mission, Arnold joined forces with Ethan Allen instead of arguing about who would be in command. He accepted his role as Allen's chief subordinate.

On the dawn of May 10th, 1775, Benedict Arnold and the Green Mountain Boys approached the slumbering fort with stealth and decisiveness. They caught the garrison by surprise, capturing the fort without loss of life. The fort's cache of artillery and munitions was enormous. From Fort Ticonderoga and Crown Point (which was captured later), the Americans seized seventy-eight cannons, six mortars, three howitzers, approximately eighteen thousand pounds of musket balls, and thirty thousand flints. The prize was more than Washington needed.[32]

Hauling It to Boston

Capturing the fort was just the beginning. The greater challenge lay in the fact that Boston was nearly three hundred miles away from Ticonderoga. The mighty task of moving massive artillery through unforgiving terrain fell to Colonel Henry Knox, the newly appointed chief of artillery for the Continental Army.

---

[32] American Battlefield Trust. (2024, February 15). Fort Ticonderoga, May 10, 1775. Retrieved from American Battlefield Trust: https://www.battlefields.org/learn/maps/fort-ticonderoga-may-10-1775.

Henry Knox, a twenty-five-year-old with no formal military training, convinced General George Washington that he could transport the sixty tons of artillery to Boston. Washington, impressed by the younger man's confidence and understanding of artillery's impact on warfare, gave Knox his blessing. With that, Knox set off on his daunting journey. He reached Fort Ticonderoga on December 5th, 1775, and the march to Boston started on December 17th.

The journey was fraught with challenges right from the start. Winter had set in, and Knox's convoy had to navigate not just roads but also bodies of water that, despite the cold, had yet to freeze over entirely. They traversed icy rivers, snowy forests, and the Berkshire Mountains with enormous sleds, oxen, and sheer grit. The condition of the roads was calamitous. Knox and his team often had to shore up bridges or dismantle the cannons and carry them piece by piece over particularly rough patches. The great weight of the cannons often caused the sleds to break through the ice. Many cannons had to be retrieved from the icy waters.

The route from Ticonderoga wound southeast to the headwaters of the Hudson River, through Albany, and across Massachusetts. The Knox Trail, as it later came to be known, is a testament to the physical and mental fortitude of those who, despite the harsh winter, pushed forward with relentless determination.

Surprisingly, the rivers served not as barriers but as aids to transport goods. Knox used boats when possible and leveraged the ice as a platform when the waters froze enough to bear the artillery's substantial weight.

After an arduous journey that lasted nearly two months, Knox's expedition reached Cambridge, Massachusetts, on January 24th, 1776, with the cannons intact. The arrival of sophisticated armaments, including cannons, mortars, and howitzers, was a significant boost to American morale and strategy. Washington now possessed the firepower to position guns on Dorchester Heights. The artillery supply train included more than fifty pieces of captured ordnance.[33]

[33] massmoments.org. (2024, February 15). Henry Knox Brings Cannon to Boston. Retrieved from massmoments.org: https://www.massmoments.org/moment-details/henry-knox-brings-cannon-to-boston.html.

Fortifying Dorchester Heights

Washington now had the artillery required to bring an end to the siege of Boston. The colonial commander in chief decided to place the cannons on Dorchester Heights.

Fortifying Dorchester Heights stands out as a masterstroke by George Washington and his army. This military operation demonstrated the ingenuity and resolve of the Continental Army and significantly altered the course of the war. Situated at a strategic military location because of its elevation, Dorchester Heights offered commanding views over the city of Boston and its harbor. Any force holding this ground could threaten ships and troop movements, a fact not lost on either side of the conflict. Understanding its significance, George Washington, who wanted to end the siege once and for all, hatched a plan to fortify this location and tighten the noose around British-occupied Boston.

Under cover of darkness, on the night of March 4th, 1776, a force of 1,200 men, including troops, laborers, and even teams of oxen, silently began the laborious task of constructing fortifications. Armed with over three hundred wagons of fascines, gabions, and prefabricated fortifications, they worked through the night under the direction of Colonel Rufus Putnam, who had proved himself an engineer of considerable talent.

Under constant threat of discovery, the American forces managed to transport and assemble artillery and build a formidable position that had been a bare hill before. Large cannons, recently transported overland from Fort Ticonderoga, were also positioned, ready to unleash their power on British-controlled areas.

The men worked with an urgency dictated by their desperation for a decisive move against the British. Their labor in the biting cold, breaking ground that was still frozen and constructing barriers destined to change the momentum of the war, was a testament to their dedication and the brilliance of Washington's calculated risk.

Their movements were so stealthy that the British sentries in Boston remained oblivious to the activities taking place just a few hundred yards away. By the dawn's light, to the shock of the British forces, Dorchester Heights bristled with fortifications.

On the morning of March 5th, British General William Howe woke to an astonishing and disheartening sight. Dorchester Heights, which had been clear the previous day, now presented an imposing military installation overlooking his positions. Reportedly, he said, "The rebels have done more in one night than my whole army would have done in a month." He quickly realized the precariousness of his situation. The newly installed American artillery had the range to inflict severe damage on his ships in the harbor and make the British hold on Boston untenable.[34]

Unable to dislodge the Americans from their newfound stronghold and unwilling to subject his forces and the loyalist population in Boston to bombardment, General Howe had little choice but to evacuate. Washington's strategic placement of forces on Dorchester Heights led directly to the British departure on March 17th, a day still remembered in Boston as Evacuation Day. On that day, the people of Boston witnessed the retreat of British troops, symbolically ending the occupancy that had started nearly eight years before with the Townshend Acts.

The successful siege effectively ended British authority in Massachusetts and set the stage for the Declaration of Independence. However, the departure of British troops did not bring immediate peace or stability to Boston. Despite the victory, the city was left in a state of economic fragility. The blockade had severely impacted trade, a cornerstone of Boston's economy.

Furthermore, a sizeable loyalist population, integrally woven into the local society and economy, had fled, leaving behind homes, shops, and an uncertain future. It took years for commerce to recover. Politically, the departure of the royal governor and his administration allowed for a new, patriot-led government to take control. The Massachusetts Provincial Congress took on greater authority, directing the war effort locally and participating in continental governance.

Boston would face challenges, but the British were gone and would not come back. Boston was now the symbol and center of the patriot cause. It swelled with an energy that fueled the spirit of independence. Washington and the Continental Army had achieved a victory that seemed impossible a few weeks before. It marked the first major military victory for the colonists.

---

[34] Boston National Historical Park. (2024, February 15). Dorchester Heights. Retrieved from Nps.org: https://www.nps.gov/places/dorchester-heights.htm.

In Summary

In retrospect, the year 1775 established the cornerstone of American military tradition. Washington's strategic patience and his willingness to employ unconventional tactics laid the foundation for future successes against the British. The Continental Army emerged from 1775 not only battle-hardened but also imbued with a sense of national identity and purpose that transcended the colonial divide. The year 1775 was only the beginning.

However, the success of the first year did not chase away the dark clouds that were forming on the horizon. The Continental Army had been victorious against a rump force used for garrison duty. Other British regiments were better and standing at the ready. Washington and his officers might have celebrated with the others on that day, but the general and his staff knew a terrible truth. The might of the British Empire had yet to be brought to bear on the Thirteen Colonies. Parliament and the British Crown would not go quietly into the night. They would draw on the considerable military resources Great Britain had and respond in force. A terrible reality would soon sail westward from the mother country.

Chapter 6: A Declaration and Invasions

A subtle push toward independence came from the British government. The Olive Branch Petition, a final effort to convince the British Crown to negotiate a reasonable resolution of differences, was firmly rejected by Parliament in August 1775. King George III refused to read it. The Thirteen Colonies declared they were in rebellion via the Proclamation of Rebellion on August 23rd, 1775.

It Was Common Sense

During the colonial period, many leaders held a philosophical view that was heavily influenced by the Enlightenment. The ideas of reason, natural rights, and people's sovereignty gave weight to the concept of independence. Colonial intellectuals drew inspiration from the works of Jean-Jacques Rousseau's *The Social Contract* and John Locke's belief in the right to life, liberty, and property. These thinkers and their writings encouraged leaders to envision a government that reflected the will of the governed, which was a radical departure from the traditional monarchy. Even ordinary citizens were beginning to desire an independent nation.

Before 1776, the concept of total independence was considered radical by many colonists, who still clung to the hope of reconciliation with the British Crown. Thomas Paine, an English-born philosopher, political activist, and revolutionary, recognized the potential of the written word to unify the colonists and how it could shift their perspective toward outright independence.

A portrait of Thomas Paine.

Common Sense, published anonymously in January 1776, was a timely and strategic masterstroke penned by Paine that crystallized the need for liberty and the immediate severance from Britain. It was direct, easily understood, and unapologetically bold. Arguing against monarchies and hereditary succession, Paine's pamphlet spoke a simple yet powerful truth to common folk, which resonated across the Thirteen Colonies.[35]

Starting with general reflections on government and religion, Paine proceeded to discuss the English constitution, the challenges of

[35] Kiger, P. J. (2023, July 11). How Thomas Paine's "Common Sense" Helped Inspire the American Revolution. Retrieved from History.com: https://www.history.com/news/thomas-paine-common-sense-revolution.

monarchial rule, and the machinations of the British monarchy toward the colonies. However, the crux of his argument lay in the notion that independence was feasible and imperative for the growth, prosperity, and preservation of the colonies' rights. Paine facilitated a robust public discourse that shifted the colonists' mindset toward a shared identity and purpose by laying simple truths out in the open.[36]

A Petition Put Forward

The petition for independence was not a hurried document. While the first rumors of independence circulated after the Battles of Lexington and Concord, it wasn't until June 7th, 1776, that Richard Henry Lee of Virginia presented a formal resolution that "these United Colonies are, and of right ought to be, free and independent States."[37]

Thomas Jefferson, who was a Virginia delegate to the Second Continental Congress, was tasked with the momentous duty of drafting the declaration. His command of language and his standing as an ardent advocate for colonial rights made him a natural choice to author the document.

It would be a difficult task. Jefferson faced the challenge of capturing the essence of the American Revolution and the nuances of political theory that were developing during that time. Jefferson patiently wrote and revised the text, distilling the shared will of all Americans into words that still reverberate today. The final draft is still considered a masterpiece.[38]

The Declaration of Independence states clearly that "all men are created equal," not just a privileged few, and all of them are "endowed by their Creator with certain unalienable rights," boldly asserting that the purpose of government is to protect these rights and that the people have the right to alter or abolish said government should it become destructive. The Declaration of Independence's ideological heft was crucial in transmuting the war for colonial rights into a global statement of human rights. Its impact would be felt around the world, inspiring

[36] Paine, T. (2024, February 17). Thomas Paine, Common Sense, 1776. Retrieved from Billofrightsinstitute.org: https://billofrightsinstitute.org/activities/thomas-paine-common-sense-1776.

[37] Lee Resolution (2022, February 8). Lee Resolution. Retrieved from National Archives: https://www.archives.gov/milestone-documents/lee-resolution.

[38] Bill of Rights Institute. (2024, February 17). Thomas Jefferson and the Declaration of Independence. Retrieved from Billofrightsinstitute.org: https://billofrightsinstitute.org/essays/thomas-jefferson-and-the-declaration-of-independence.

future independence movements.

The Ensuing Floor Debate

The draft of the Declaration of Independence was examined and reviewed by the Second Continental Congress with a critical eye. There were debates about including the concept of inalienable rights, which was a novel idea at the time. The Declaration of Independence's statement of "life, liberty, and the pursuit of happiness" had to defend its place in democratic discourse.

The discussions were not mere semantics; they were serious debates about the over-empowerment of the executive branch over the legislative and judicial branches. There was also significant debate about the legality of the slave trade.

It is essential to reflect on these debates because they reveal the cautious approach of the Congress and the diverse philosophical currents that underpinned the American Revolution. Ultimately, the argument for independence prevailed, branding King George a tyrant and asserting colonial sovereignty. However, the approval of the Declaration of Independence took time and effort. Because of John Adams's, Benjamin Franklin's diplomacy, and the spirit of those who dared to envision a new republic, the obstacles of indecision and internal strife were overcome, one deliberative step at a time.

Following a final revision and a vote for independence, the Declaration of Independence was formally adopted on July 4th, 1776, but not without controversy. Some delegates hesitated, and others withheld their signatures. There was the lingering belief that the rift with Britain could be mended. The final act of signing the Declaration of Independence on August 2nd, 1776, was not merely ceremonial; it symbolized a crossing of the Rubicon into the unsettling yet undeniably exhilarating frontier of nationhood.[39]

The delegates were aware of the risks. The British had shown in the past, notably during the Jacobite rising of 1745, how they would deal with rebels and their families. The delegates signed, knowing they might all hang separately or together.

---

[39] National Geographic. (2024, February 17). Signing of the Declaration of Independence. Retrieved from Education.nationalgeographic.org: https://education.nationalgeographic.org/resource/signing-declaration-independence/.

The Declaration of Independence is a document that has spurred civil rights movements, guided global ideologues, and set the template for national aspirations. Its words have echoed across diverse landscapes, acting as a beacon for the oppressed and a challenge to the status quo.

However, the story of its creation is a tale of ideological clashes and the evolution of political thought. The Declaration of Independence is more than just a piece of paper; it is the collective thoughts of a nation being born, and its legacy continues to guide us.

The Musings of the Stagirite

A sad irony about the Declaration of Independence is that it speaks of liberty, but there were delegates of the Second Continental Congress who were slaveholders. There appears to be a conflict between beliefs that advocate freedom but consider bondage acceptable.

We know that the Founding Fathers were influenced by Locke's and Rousseau's writings on liberty. Still, there was another philosopher, considered one of the greatest, whose opinions were held in high esteem and whose thoughts were probably considered. His name was Aristotle.

Aristotle's teachings laid the foundation for many disciplines and had a significant impact on the understanding of polis or the city-state and its governance. Aristotle defends the idea of slavery in his work, *Politics*.[40]

For Aristotle, slavery (*doulos* in Greek) was a natural institution. He believed that some individuals were "slaves by nature," attributing this status to those who lacked the ability to reason and govern themselves. In his view, the polis was the highest form of community, with governance reflecting familial dynamics. A master's rule over his slave mimics a ruler's dominion over his subjects. To Aristotle, a just polis would entail a just relationship between masters and those who were slaves. He further believed that slavery was a natural condition and that there were those who were born as natural slaves, likening them to "living tools" or domestic animals. He was not alone in his musings. Plato thought that those who were better had the right to rule over the inferior.

Aristotle's influence on the American Revolution might not have been dominant, but his writings are part of the Western canon. Even though people like Thomas Jefferson, who proclaimed that "all men are

---

[40] UKessays.com. (2024, February 17). Aristotle's Views on Slavery. Retrieved from UKessays.com: https://www.ukessays.com/essays/politics/slavery.php.

created equal," were influenced by Enlightenment thought, they were also products of an environment steeped in the Aristotelian tradition.[41]

Attacking North

The invasion of Canada did not happen in isolation, and it was not a spontaneous event. It was part of a strategy that would spread the American Revolutionary War beyond the borders of the Thirteen Colonies. The Province of Quebec was a British stronghold, and the Continental Army believed that by seizing Canada, they could safeguard the northern flank of the colonies and persuade their northern neighbors to join the fight against the British. Success would require the British to spread their armed forces and limit military action against the Thirteen Colonies.

The offensive began in September 1775. Major General Richard Montgomery launched the campaign from Fort Ticonderoga with approximately 1,700 men (the American force would eventually grow to more than 10,000 soldiers). Meanwhile, Benedict Arnold led 1,100 Continental troops from Massachusetts through the state of Maine. Montgomery marched toward Montreal, and Arnold headed toward Quebec City. The overall plan was ambitious: enter Quebec, convince Canadians to support the revolution, and neutralize British influence in the region.

Early Success

In November, Montgomery successfully reached Fort St. Jean, located outside Montreal. This achievement convinced Sir Guy Carleton, the royal governor, to retreat to Quebec, leading to the evacuation of Montreal. The Americans took control of Montreal on November 28th. Meanwhile, Benedict Arnold had made his way through the forests of Maine and had arrived outside Quebec. In December, Montgomery joined Arnold, who then passed his command to the senior officer.

The Americans assaulted Quebec's fortifications on December 31st during a snowstorm but were eventually pushed back. General Montgomery was killed in the attack. Benedict Arnold tried to continue the siege, but in the spring, British reinforcements under General John Burgoyne arrived. The Americans finally left Montreal on May 9th, 1776,

---

[41] BBC.com. (2024, February 17). Philosophers Justifying Slavery. Retrieved from Ethics guide: https://www.bbc.co.uk/ethics/slavery/ethics/philosophers_1.shtml.

and eventually made it back to New York. The dream of a fourteenth colony with Canada joining the fight for independence from British rule faded into the background. The Continental Army refocused its efforts on battles to the south.[42]

The Death of General Montgomery in the Attack on Quebec, December 31, 1775, by John Trumbull.
https://en.wikipedia.org/wiki/File:The_Death_of_General_Montgomery_in_the_Attack_on_Quebec_December_31_1775.jpeg

While the invasion did not succeed in its ultimate goals, it still played a significant part in the broader theatrics of the American Revolutionary War. It highlighted the tactical and logistical challenges of wartime operations and exemplified the unpredictability of alliances and colonial relationships.

For Americans, it highlighted the limitations of their military might and the necessity for strategic diplomacy. For Canadians, it fostered a sense of unity and reinforced their allegiance to the British Crown, a sentiment that would shape Canada's national identity for years to come.

The British Have Come

The Continental Army returned from the Canadian fiasco but had little time to lick its wounds. An event of devastating proportions was

[42] Sprague, D. (2023, January 24). American Revolution and Canada. Retrieved from Thecanadianencyclopedia.ca: https://www.thecanadianencyclopedia.ca/en/article/american-revolution.

about to happen in New York City. The British returned, and they came in full force. The British invasion of New York in 1776 stands as a pivotal moment in the American Revolutionary War, marking both an escalation in the young conflict and a crucial test for the Continental Army under General George Washington.

The British invasion of New York was born out of strategic necessity. With New York's harbors offering strategic naval advantages and the city serving as a nexus of commerce and communication, the British command recognized the immense value of controlling it. Control over New York would sever the line of communication between the northern and southern colonies, thus hindering the unity and effectiveness of the colonial resistance.

It was an 18th-century exercise in shock and awe. On June 29th, 1776, witnesses reported seeing hundreds of British ships crowding the horizon, a stark premonition of the vast military force that sought to crush the burgeoning rebellion. The fleet itself consisted of hundreds of ships, among them warships that far outclassed any naval firepower held by the Continental forces. The army component of the invasion was somewhere between thirty thousand and forty-five thousand troops, including Hessian mercenaries hired from the German states.

The high command was a family affair. Sir William Howe returned as the army commander, no doubt anxious to make up for his embarrassment at Boston. The impressive British armada was captained by his brother, Admiral Richard Howe, who was not only a seasoned naval commander but also an appointed peace commissioner by the Crown. He had a dual mandate to both quell the rebellion and negotiate with its leaders.

It would take some time for the massive force to gather, but the British were not worried about an attack from an American fleet. Admiral Howe's fleet arrived at Staten Island on July 12th and began to unload troops and supplies. Another British fleet showed up on August 12th, and a third arrived on August 15th. The British eventually had thirty-two thousand soldiers and ten thousand sailors on Staten Island. This was the largest amphibious assault in European history up to that time.[43]

---

[43] Revolutionary-war-and-beyond.com. (2024, February 24). Admiral Howe's Fleet Arrives at Staten Island. Retrieved from Revolutionary-war-and-beyond.com: https://www.revolutionary-war-and-beyond.com/admiral-howes-fleet-arrives-staten-island.html.

The American Defense

General George Washington was not caught unawares. Anticipating the move, he had already begun fortifying defenses around New York City, particularly on Brooklyn Heights, which offered a commanding position over the East River. Washington's strategy hinged on the defense of strategic points like Fort Washington on Manhattan Island and Fort Lee across the river in New Jersey. However, Washington's defensive resources were considerably stretched, and his forces lacked the experience of their British counterparts.

There were also lingering doubts about the loyalties of the city's inhabitants, many of whom were divided in their sentiments toward the patriot cause. Washington was confronted with the possibility of a group supplying intelligence to the Howe brothers.

The Battle of Long Island

Howe wasted no time in preparing his troops for battle against the Continental Army. The two armies faced each other on August 22nd, 1776, in what is known as the Battle of Long Island or the Battle of Brooklyn. The British army had a significant advantage in men and naval power, with approximately twenty thousand well-trained and equipped soldiers supported by a powerful fleet. In contrast, the American forces comprised roughly ten thousand soldiers from the Continental Army and local militias with varying levels of experience and equipment. Washington's troops were spread thin across defensive positions in Brooklyn and Manhattan.

The British executed a well-planned attack, circumventing American fortifications by marching through the Jamaica Pass to attack the Continental Army from the rear, which caught the Americans off-guard. Fierce fighting ensued, particularly around Gowanus Road and Guan Heights. Despite brave resistance, the American forces were outmaneuvered and in danger of being encircled. As casualties mounted, the situation grew dire.

The battle culminated in a decisive British victory. While the exact number of casualties remains debated, estimates suggest that the Americans suffered significant losses, with hundreds killed and up to a thousand captured. The British, while victorious, incurred lighter casualties.

However, the Continental Army was not destroyed. In the face of overwhelming odds, General Washington's leadership shone through.

Under cover of darkness and with the aid of some lucky fog, he ordered a strategic retreat. The evacuation across the East River to Manhattan was executed with such secrecy and efficiency that it preserved the core of the Continental Army. It would live to fight another day.[44]

The Fight for Manhattan

After the Continental Army's evacuation from Long Island, General Washington knew Manhattan would be the next target for the British forces. The Continental Army fortified positions on the island, yet Washington was apprehensive about the defense of the city due to its geographical vulnerabilities.

There was still some hope for a peaceful resolution. Notably, during this period, a peace conference was held on September 11th, 1776, with the Staten Island Peace Conference. However, these attempts failed, as the American delegates, including Benjamin Franklin and John Adams, rejected the British demand for unconditional loyalty to the British Crown.

With peace negotiations at an impasse, combat became inevitable. The following engagements happened in the following weeks:

- **The Landing at Kip's Bay** (September 15th): A British force commanded by General William Howe landed unopposed, forcing an American retreat.

- **The Harlem Heights Encounter** (September 16th): The Continental Army engaged with British forces in a skirmish that, while minor in scale, boosted the morale of American forces.

- **The Battle of White Plains** (October 28th): This engagement saw Washington's troops holding their lines against a superior force until they withdrew.

The military situation changed dramatically on October 18th when four thousand British troops landed at Pelham to outflank the Continental Army. Washington decided to evacuate Manhattan, but he was persuaded by General Nathanael Greene to keep a garrison at Fort Washington, located at the northern tip of Manhattan. Those remaining troops would prevent the British from following Washington as the Continental Army escaped. Washington agreed and left Colonel Robert

---

[44] Mark, H. W. (2024, January 25). Battle of Long Island. Retrieved from Worldhistory.com: https://www.worldhistory.org/article/2359/battle-of-long-island/.

Magaw with three thousand men.

<u>The Defense of Fort Washington</u>

Fort Washington was a crucial location due to its position. It had a commanding view of the Hudson River, which allowed it to control the vital waterway alongside its twin fortress, Fort Lee, situated across the river in New Jersey. The Continental Army fought bravely to defend Fort Washington, but it ended in a tragic outcome. The fort was surrounded and overwhelmed by a larger British force that was equipped with artillery. As a result, the fort fell on November 16th, 1776, leading to the capture of nearly three thousand American troops. However, although unsuccessful, the tenacious defense by the colonial forces demonstrated that they would not surrender easily, defying British expectations of a quick end to the rebellion.

The British now had complete control of New York City and would remain there until the end of the war. General William Howe technically won the campaign to take the city, but he made some tactical errors. On Staten Island, Howe missed a critical opportunity to destroy Washington's army before it could solidify its position in Manhattan. Howe's hesitation allowed Washington to evacuate his troops and regroup, a decision that some historians assert prolonged the war.

Once in Manhattan, Howe again demonstrated his cautious nature by not aggressively pursuing the retreating American forces after their defeat at Fort Washington. His failure to capitalize on his victories gave Washington the chance to retreat and fight another day. Howe beat the Continental Army, but he did not destroy it.[45]

<u>Winter Weather</u>

Undoubtedly, the British in New York City must have chuckled about the Declaration of Independence. Their army had been the winner on the battlefield. The Continental Army was in disarray, and its soldiers were running for their lives across New York and New Jersey. The final capitulation of the rebels would happen in a couple of weeks.

Meanwhile, snowy weather was coming, and the British soldiers and officers were settling into their winter quarters and looking forward to a welcome vacation of a few months. There would be parties, balls,

---

[45] Mark, H. W. (2024, February 1). New York and New Jersey Campaign. Retrieved from Worldhistory.com: https://www.worldhistory.org/article/2364/new-york-and-new-jersey-campaign/.

dinners, and other festive occasions. There were so many delightful things to occupy the minds of the British generals.

Washington and his ragged band of ruffians were about to spring a surprise on the unsuspecting British.

Chapter 7: The Miracles of Trenton and Saratoga

Major General Charles Cornwallis (First Marquess Cornwallis) was sent in pursuit of the fleeing Continental Army after the Americans left New York City. Claiming that he would catch Washington the way a hunter catches a fox, Cornwallis marched with a column of ten thousand soldiers across the wintery countryside. Thanks to the stubborn resistance of Fort Washington, the Continental Army had a head start. George Washington was able to stay one step ahead of the hounds.

He did this with an army whose ranks were depleted by disease and desertion. Washington knew a pitched battle with the pursuing British would be suicide. The American commander adopted a Fabian strategy: he would keep evading the British until time and circumstances allowed him to fight on better terms. This meant he would continue to retreat until the right moment arrived for him to fight. Others criticized his decision, but it allowed Washington to preserve his forces and position them opportunistically for future engagements.

A few weeks passed, and then an opportunity arose. Washington had the Delaware River between him and the British.

Cornwallis stopped his pursuit and placed his men in winter quarters. It was a military custom practiced by European armies, and the British would not fight unless necessary. Washington knew he could launch a surprise attack, so he went after the Hessians encamped at Trenton, New

Jersey.[46]

Hessian Mercenaries

The Hessians were German soldiers hired by the British as mercenaries. This practice provided various small German states with much-needed funds and military activity for their surplus soldiers. Hessians were predominantly recruited from the Hesse-Kassel state but included individuals from other German principalities. Recruitment into Hessian service was not always voluntary. Many of these soldiers were "spirited away"—a euphemism for involuntary drafting. Their journey across the Atlantic was not just a voyage toward war but also a bitter separation from their homeland.

They were tough, disciplined soldiers with a reputation for ferocious fighting. Striking them was not without serious risk, and they had to be taken by surprise. Washington had that in mind as he prepared to recross the Delaware River in the early hours of December 26th, 1776.

The Crossing

Washington's master plan brewed over weeks, a careful concoction of intelligence gathering, troop management, and the hope that the winter weather could keep his strategy veiled from the overly confident British.

The Americans secured all available watercraft on the Delaware River. These included Durham cargo boats, which had shallow drafts and were forty to sixty feet long. The Durham boats would ferry across the soldiers while flat-bottomed ferries would bring across the artillery and horses. New Englanders from Marblehead, Massachusetts, provided the labor to row the boats across the Delaware. The crossing commenced the night of December 25th.[47]

Washington led his weary but resolute soldiers in a treacherous crossing. The elements were as much a foe as the British, but the inclement weather also played a hand in Washington's favor. The driving snow and freezing conditions kept the Hessian garrison in Trenton numb with cold and complacent in their security.

---

[46] Mark, H. W. (2024, February 1). New York and New Jersey Campaign. Retrieved from Worldhistory.com: https://www.worldhistory.org/article/2364/new-york-and-new-jersey-campaign/.

[47] Mountvernon.org. (2024, February 21). 10 Facts About Washington's Crossing of the Delaware River. Retrieved from George Washington's Mount Vernon: https://www.mountvernon.org/george-washington/the-revolutionary-war/washingtons-revolutionary-war-battles/the-trenton-princeton-campaign/10-facts-about-washingtons-crossing-of-the-delaware-river/.

The crossing was a tactical marvel. The where, the when, and the how were all perfectly executed. Once across, the Continental Army had to march ten miles to Trenton. They reached Trenton by 8:00 a.m. and advanced in two columns. Fortunately, the Hessians had been carousing the night before. None of them expected to be attacked.

The Hessians never saw it coming. Within ninety minutes, Washington and his men had secured Trenton. Several hundred Hessians escaped, but almost one thousand of the mercenaries were captured. Four Americans were killed in what was a total victory.[48]

Inspired Leadership

The victory was the result of a combination of discipline and professionalism. Washington's move was not just strategic but also tactical. His careful planning included ensuring the discipline of his forces in the aftermath of the battle. It would have been easy for him to lose self-control, but Washington knew that showing restraint and order would amplify the respect for the new American army and their cause. It was a tremendous morale boost, and Washington desperately needed that.

After the Battle of Trenton, Washington addressed the troops whose enlistments would expire on December 31st at the stroke of midnight. Washington begged them to stay at least one more month. His request resulted in two hundred men volunteering to reenlist at that moment.

Princeton

Washington was not finished with the British that winter. He made the strategic decision to press on, aiming to attack and rout a British garrison at nearby Princeton, further unnerving the British forces and solidifying patriot gains. By using bold, deceptive tactics and precisely timing his movements, Washington caught a brigade of British regulars off-guard.

On the morning of January 3rd, 1777, Washington's army, which now numbered over five thousand with reenlistments and new volunteers, faced off against approximately eight thousand British regulars. As the armies met, a dense fog settled over the battlefield, providing cover for Washington's men as they clashed with the British. The engagement was fierce, with both sides fighting tenaciously. Under the command of

---

[48] History.com. (2024, February 21). George Washington Crosses the Delaware. Retrieved from History.com: https://www.history.com/this-day-in-history/washington-crosses-the-delaware.

Generals Hugh Mercer and John Cadwalader, the Americans managed to blunt assaults by British regulars and Hessian mercenaries.

The turning point came when Washington led a charge against British forces from the rear, a brash and bold move. The British, believing they had the upper hand, were taken by surprise and soon outmaneuvered. They found themselves in a retreat as Washington's troops gained the field.

The American victory at Princeton was a strategic success that vastly outstripped the Continental Army's original objectives. The Continental Army had managed to outmaneuver and outfight the British, an army considered to be the best in the world. The casualties were relatively light, but the impact was immeasurable.[49]

The Aftermath of Victories

The Battles of Trenton and Princeton sent shockwaves through the British and Hessian commands. They were forced to reassess the American forces, recognizing that they were not simply rebels but a cunning and determined adversary. These shocks rippled through the British grand strategy, impacting their tactics and the overconfidence that had plagued them in the early stages of the war. The British decision to hunker down in New York after their defeats rather than pursue further conflicts demonstrated the resounding impact these battles had on the revolution's broader dynamics.

The morale within the Continental Army, once on the cusp of collapse, now surged with life. The news of the victory resonated throughout the Thirteen Colonies, attracting additional volunteers to the Continental Army.

The ripple effect of these two victories was felt in the hearts and minds of the American people, forging a determination to see the war through to its conclusion. Trenton and Princeton were not just military victories; they were triumphs of the underdog, a validation of the American cause, and a turning point in the conflict.

Trenton and Princeton embodied the spirit of the American Revolution–the tenacity to fight for one's beliefs, to innovate in the face of overwhelming odds, and to seize opportunities where none seemingly exist. The lessons of flexibility, audacity, and strategic vision that

---

[49] Rosenfield, R. (2024, February 21). Princeton. Retrieved from Battlefields.org: https://www.battlefields.org/learn/articles/princeton.

emerged from these two engagements serve as inspirations for generations of American leaders and military tacticians.

There was more to come in the new year. The year 1777 was the scene of the most decisive battle of the American Revolution.

Gentleman Johnny's Strategy

John Burgoyne was an aristocrat stuck in the American backwoods. He was more familiar with the corridors of power back in London than the wilds of the North American continent. Famous for his wit and charm, Burgoyne was a frequent figure in the social circles of England. He was equally at home composing plays as he was plotting campaigns.

In 1777, Burgoyne was placed in command of a scheme that, if successful, would split the new American nation.

A portrait of John Burgoyne.
https://commons.wikimedia.org/wiki/File:BurgoyneByReynolds.jpg

Saratoga Campaign

It was an innovative idea. Burgoyne's strategy was to divide the rebel colonies and isolate New England geographically. His campaign was bold—advance south from Canada, link forces with British troops in New York City, and split the colonies in half.

The plan looked great on paper. Burgoyne proposed a three-pronged pincer move, expecting support from British forces moving northward and up the Hudson River from New York City. His immediate goal was to capture Albany, a key colonial city, and secure a portion of upstate New York, which was known for its divisiveness and potential loyalist support.

The campaign had several key goals:

- Securing the allegiance of Native American tribes.
- Ensuring supply lines to British-controlled North America.
- Leveraging Canadian loyalists to form a substantial fighting force.

The Hudson Valley was an appealing route. Control of the Hudson River meant control of a vital artery for the movement of arms and supplies, as well as a means to effectively divide and manage the colonies, which was a desired goal of British military planners.

For Burgoyne, the Hudson represented the promised land, replete with the spoils of war and the glory of conquest. Gentleman Johnny, as he was known, forgot some key elements, though. In pursuing his goals, he failed to fully comprehend the difficulties of the terrain and the determination of the colonial forces defending it.

An Elaborate Pincer Move

The Saratoga Campaign had three movements coming from separate starting points. General Burgoyne commanded the northern pincer and was the central assault force. Burgoyne commanded a force of approximately eight thousand soldiers, some freshly transported from England, others drawn from those already stationed in North America. Burgoyne's army started south in June 1777. Its first objective was Fort Ticonderoga.

The western pincer was under the command of Lieutenant Colonel Matthew "Barry" St. Leger. His 1,600 troops were a mix of British regulars, Hessians, Native Americans, Canadians, and loyalists. St. Leger would move through the Mohawk Valley from Lake Ontario and act as a diversion before joining with Burgoyne in Albany. A force from the south under General William Howe would advance from New York City to meet Burgoyne in Albany. Everything looked great on paper, but things gradually fell apart.[50]

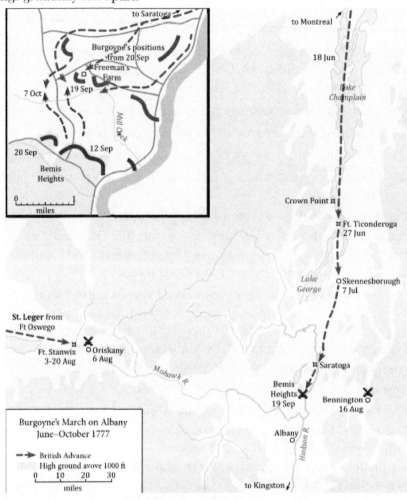

Burgoyne's march on Albany.

Logistical Problems

Burgoyne quickly captured Fort Ticonderoga, and his troops were steadily moving south in August. St. Leger besieged Fort Stanwix. Everything looked promising. That is about the time when things started to go wrong.

---

[50] Bill, R. (2021, August 4). The Northern Campaign of 1777. Retrieved from Nps.gov: https://www.nps.gov/fost/blogs/the-northern-campaign-of-1777.htm.

Burgoyne assumed a much larger populace of loyalists on the path from Ticonderoga to Albany, a mistake that led to insufficient intelligence about enemy dispositions and support. He expected a wave of support from local loyalists that never materialized, depriving him of crucial local knowledge and aid. Burgoyne's progress required extensive supply lines over rugged terrain, and logistics were not given the same attention as the grand strategic strokes of his campaign.

In the 18th century, the Hudson Valley was a rugged, inhospitable landscape dotted with thick forests, swamps, and treacherous mountains. The lack of infrastructure and the terrain's intimidating nature magnified the campaign's challenges. The British logistical system was designed for European warfare, where supply was less of an issue. In the American wilderness, however, the system struggled to keep pace, leading to shortages of food and ammunition. Wagons and draught animals, vital for mobility and life support, were lost at a worrying rate to the harsh conditions and enemy attacks.

Burgoyne's supply lines from Canada were tenuous at best, and his army was forced to rely heavily on foraging and requisitioning local provisions. This approach alienated the local population, sapped the army's strength, and made deterring Native American scalping parties a pressing concern. As Burgoyne's forces moved farther from their base, they became increasingly isolated and vulnerable. The worst challenge the flamboyant British commander faced was an opponent who refused to back down from British military might.

The American Resistance

The Americans did not follow a European plan. They learned from the Native Americans about how to use the land to their advantage. As the British moved south, the Americans put a strategy of attrition to work. They destroyed crops, burned bridges, and harassed the British flanks. This constant pressure disrupted the supply chain and sowed seeds of discontent among British soldiers already enduring exhausting conditions.

Marauding bands led by statesmen and soldiers like Seth Warner and John Stark encapsulated the spirit of defiance. Utilizing their intimate knowledge of the local terrain, they engaged in hit-and-run tactics, keeping the British on their toes and creating a sense of insecurity within their ranks.

There were instances where the Americans stood and fought. The Battle of Hubbardton pitted the Continental troops against British forces. The Americans were tactically outmaneuvered but managed a successful withdrawal. The British suffered a delayed advance and significant casualties.

American Commanders

The Continental Army was led by highly competent commanders who guided their troops with skill and ingenuity during this campaign.

General Philip Schuyler was the original commander tasked with fortifying the Hudson River against the British. A respected leader both on the battlefield and in the political arena, Schuyler's character was marked by his unyielding commitment to the cause of American independence. His leadership was characterized by a deep sense of duty and an unwavering dedication to safeguarding the principles of the revolution. Horatio Gates replaced him.

A portrait of Horatio Gates.
https://commons.wikimedia.org/wiki/File:HoratioGatesByStuart_crop.jpg

A veteran of the British army before joining the Continental Army, General Horatio Gates's command style was marked by meticulous planning and caution. His character was the exact opposite of Benedict Arnold, his mercurial subordinate. Benedict Arnold's primary role was assembling the forces to halt Burgoyne's advance. Though ultimately controversial, Arnold's unorthodox tactics and sheer audacity demonstrated the value of thinking outside the conventional military playbook.

The American commanders' ability to be adaptable and creative in their approach contributed significantly to the efforts made to frustrate the British.

The Demise of St. Leger

The first sign that the Saratoga Campaign would be a British failure was at Fort Stanwix. St. Leger began the siege on August 2nd, but contrary to expectations, the garrison refused to surrender and stubbornly resisted. St. Leger received false information that Benedict Arnold was coming with three thousand men to relieve the fort (Arnold only had seven hundred men with him). St. Leger believed the report and, on August 22nd, abandoned the siege of Fort Stanwix. That permitted the Americans to concentrate more on destroying Burgoyne's advance.

The Advance to Disaster

Burgoyne's column continued to push through the natural obstacles and enemy attacks. The British endured a defeat at the Battle of Bennington on August 16th but were still moving south toward Albany. General Gates moved north on September 7th to oppose the British and created fortifications at Bemis Heights.

General Howe's Choice

William Howe was an intriguing figure. There were times when his tactical prowess achieved great success, such as the Battle of Long Island, but there were times when his cautious behavior created serious problems. A decision he made during the Saratoga Campaign would effectively doom John Burgoyne. Howe chose to launch a major assault against Philadelphia. He advised Burgoyne of this decision on July 17th in a secret dispatch. Howe's decision isolated Burgoyne, but the latter pressed on in hopes of still making it to Albany. That forward progress was stopped fifty miles away from New York's future capital.[51]

---

[51] Howe, W. (2024, February 1). William Howe Goes His Own Way. Retrieved from

Saratoga, The Final Act

Burgoyne's army was demoralized, but it was still a professional fighting force. He had lost most of his Native American allies and had almost no field intelligence to work with. The Americans were blocking the road, and Burgoyne had no alternative but to engage his enemy and hope for the best.

The Battles of Saratoga represent a poignant chapter in the story of the United States. The Saratoga region of New York was a formidable battleground. The densely forested area, broken by occasional clearings and twisting waterways, presented challenges and opportunities for both sides. Control of terrain and the high ground, in particular, would prove vital to the outcome of the conflict.

The first encounter was at Freeman's Farm on September 19th. As the British attempted to flank the American positions, an engagement ensued. The two armies clashed with ferocity, each side exchanging volleys and bayonets. It was technically a British victory, but the Americans were able to stop the British advance. The next battle would be the decisive one.[52]

Bemis Heights

The terrain at Bemis Heights was rugged, a challenge that the American forces under General Horatio Gates and his subordinate, General Benedict Arnold, would use to their advantage. What happened at Bemis Heights was a lesson in strategic warfare that saw the Americans use the landscape and innovative tactics to secure a critical victory.

The British, led by the resolute but increasingly embattled Burgoyne, sought to break through the American lines with a direct assault up the slopes of Bemis Heights. The heart of the American defense was a redoubt known as Balcarres Redoubt, a strategic strongpoint that would bear the brunt of the British assaults. As the redcoats charged the heavily fortified position, they were met with firepower that all but broke their resolve. The tactical maneuvers on both sides, including feints and envelopments, ultimately swung the advantage in favor of the Americans. General Simon Fraser, Burgoyne's best field officer, was killed by

Clements.umoich.edu: https://clements.umich.edu/exhibit/spy-letters-of-the-american-revolution/stories-of-spies/howe-goes-his-own-way/
[52] Maloy, M. (2024, February 21). The Battle of Freeman's Farm: September 19, 1777. Retrieved from Battlefields.org: https://www.battlefields.org/learn/articles/battle-freemans-farm-september-19-1777.

American sharpshooters. Throughout the battle, General Benedict Arnold emerged as a catalyst for the American cause, his brilliant leadership and personal courage inspiring his troops to superlative feats of arms.

The outcome of the Battle of Bemis Heights was the strategic withdrawal of General Burgoyne's forces to Saratoga, where they found themselves surrounded. Burgoyne knew the fight was over. After several days of negotiations, General Burgoyne surrendered on October 17th. His army of over six thousand men and forty-two artillery pieces were placed in American custody. The campaign effectively ended Burgoyne's military career and cast a long shadow over his reputation.

The surrender at Saratoga was a devastating blow to British morale and a turning point in the war. It convinced France to formally enter the conflict on the side of the Americans, a decision that would have profound implications for the war's outcome. America was about to gain some valuable allies.

Chapter 8: Allies and Adversaries

The story of France and the American Revolution is filled with political maneuvering, strategic alliances, and the hope for a new world order. From initial covert assistance to a full-fledged partnership, the journey France undertook to support the fledgling United States was fraught with risks and had some benefits for both countries.

France watched the growing conflict with a mix of interest and caution. The causes of the American rebellion echoed the burgeoning calls for reform and revolution in France. Yet, initial French involvement was minimal, mainly consisting of covert aid in the form of munitions and funds provided by private citizens, most notably from the Marquis de Lafayette and the polymathic researcher Pierre Beaumarchais.

Brothers to the Rebels

The Marquis de Lafayette is a central figure in the early relationship between France and the United States. Driven by his own ambitions for military glory and a genuine belief in the American cause, Lafayette's private lobbying of French leaders became instrumental in securing French support.

Beaumarchais, a skilled political operative who counted playwriting and inventing among his many talents, orchestrated clandestine arms deals that funneled French support to American revolutionaries. His most significant scheme, conducted under the Comte de Vergennes, involved the creation of a fictitious company, Roderigue Hortalez and Company, which provided the colonies with the crucial resources they needed to sustain their war effort. Yet, despite these individual efforts, the French government maintained an official stance of neutrality; it was wary of provoking its perennial adversary, Great Britain.

The Marquis de Lafayette wearing the uniform of an American general.
https://commons.wikimedia.org/wiki/File:Marquis_de_Lafayette_2.jpg

The Efforts of Ben Franklin

The victory at Saratoga transformed French hesitancy into a resounding yes to send aid. The American delegation, led by Benjamin Franklin, managed to secure the Treaty of Alliance with France in 1778. As a seasoned diplomat, Franklin's negotiations were instrumental in securing French support. His skillful navigation of French politics, such as leveraging the country's own motivations for weakening the British Empire, demonstrated the careful art of diplomatic finesse. The Treaty of Alliance pledged military support and financial and diplomatic backing that would prove vital to the American cause.

Settling a Few Scores

French intervention in the American Revolution was not entirely based on idealism or kind feelings for the Americans. France had a barely concealed agenda.

Few rivalries have been as brooding and long-standing as the Franco-British feud. From the Hundred Years' War to the later Napoleonic Wars, these two mighty nations seemed fated to clash time and time again. Even today, echoes of their rivalry reverberate through international relations.

The 18th century brought about colonial expansion and the rise of the global British Empire, casting a long shadow over France's imperial ambitions. As France sought to reassert its dominance and recoup its losses, it was at odds with the burgeoning power across the English Channel.

The American Revolution marked a pivotal moment in the Franco-British feud. For France, the conflict was not solely about supporting the American cause for independence; it was also an opportunity to undermine the British Empire. Unwittingly, the American colonies became a battleground for two of the most formidable military forces of the time. France did not want to weaken Great Britain, but it did want to redress the balance of power in Europe and secure its own interests.

France's entry into the American Revolution was not without its costs. France's internal economic strains from decades of royal excess were exacerbated by financial support for the American Revolution, contributing to the economic crisis that ultimately led to the overthrow of King Louis XVI and the fall of the ancien régime. It also created an alliance between France and the United States that continues to this day.[53]

Spanish Involvement

While France's contribution to the United States' struggle for independence is well documented, it is equally important to recognize the support of other allies. Spain's role tends to be overshadowed, cloaked in the shadows of the more glory-laden French alliance. However, Spain's assistance to America was pivotal, if indirect.

Spain was a major colonial power with vast territories in the Americas, including the Caribbean, Louisiana, and Florida, and possessed strategic interests in North America. Internationally, Spain was recovering from

---

[53] McGee, S. (2023, August 25). 5 Ways the French Helped Win the American Revolution. Retrieved from History.com: https://www.history.com/news/american-revolution-french-role-help.

economic woes and was intent on regaining its footing as a formidable global empire.

Spain initially maintained a stance of neutrality in the conflict between the American colonies and Great Britain, but as the war progressed, it saw an opportunity to weaken its old adversary. Under the leadership of King Charles III, Spain secretly but systematically supported the American forces, sending arms, ammunition, and financial aid. Furthermore, Spain's diplomats, such as Diego de Gardoqui, were instrumental in forging an alliance to guarantee Spanish assistance to the revolutionaries. This diplomatic coup fortified the Second Continental Congress's resolve and maneuvered Spain into a more influential position on the world stage.

Under Admiral Luis de Córdova y Córdova, the Spanish fleet played a pivotal role in critical naval engagements supporting the American cause. Spanish troops, led by Bernardo de Gálvez, undertook successful military campaigns against the British, securing important victories in the Gulf Coast and the Mississippi Valley. Gálvez's efforts were noteworthy, as his forces helped ward off British advances and facilitated coordination between Spanish, French, and American troops.

The post-war negotiations bore the fruit of Spain's calculated support for the American colonies during the war. The Treaty of Paris, signed in 1783, secured territorial gains for Spain, including control over Florida and the Mississippi River, which opened up new opportunities for Spanish expansion in North America. This was a defining moment for Spain, marking both a diplomatic triumph and an expansion of its imperial reach.[54]

The Dutch Presence

There is an unsung hero in the tale of American revolutionary support: the Netherlands, or the Dutch Republic as it was known in the 18th century. This maritime nation played a little-known but crucial role in the American War of Independence.

In the 1770s, the Dutch Republic was a fading titan in European power politics. Its navy had once been the envy of the world, and its trade, especially with its vast East India and West India companies, had

---

[54] Museum of the American Revolution. (2024, February 18). Spain and the American Revolution. Retrieved from Amrevmuseum.org: https://www.amrevmuseum.org/spain-and-the-american-revolution.

made its merchants astoundingly wealthy. However, by the time of the American Revolution, the Dutch Republic was navigating treacherous diplomatic waters. It was a relatively small, strategically located nation surrounded by larger, more aggressive powers.

The Dutch had historic ties with America since the days of the New Amsterdam colony (modern-day New York). When the American colonies rebelled against British rule, the Dutch found themselves in a difficult position. Their economy benefited from trade with the British, and they were wary of provoking a conflict that their military might be ill-prepared for. Yet, there was a potent undercurrent of Dutch sympathizers who saw America's struggle echo their own fight for independence from Spain in the 16th century.

The Dutch Republic excelled in financing wars, something it had done for centuries with the strategic use of bonds and loans. When the American colonies sought financial backing for their war effort, they turned to the Dutch and found willing lenders. The Dutch financiers saw a potentially profitable investment in the colonies with potentially high returns if America emerged successful.[55]

While officially neutral, Dutch merchants proved critical in smuggling goods to American revolutionaries. The port city of Amsterdam, in particular, became a hotspot for a variety of contraband, from weapons to tobacco. Dutch officials were often complicit, as were those in other European nations who had a vested interest in the success of the American rebels. The Dutch Republic's quiet support for America's quest for freedom illustrates how the actions of even the most minor players can have an impact.

British International Arrogance

British diplomacy during the 18th century was a delicate web of alliances and betrayals. The heart of the matter lay in the simmering dissatisfaction among the French, Spanish, and Dutch elite against the British Empire and its ambitions to redraw colonial boundaries. Armed with a powerful navy and burgeoning imperial reach, Great Britain often wielded a domineering hand.

Historians speculate why Great Britain's diplomacy became a mixture of arrogance and hubris. Some suggest that British actions resulted from

---

[55] Jstor.org. (2024, February 18). Foreign Intervention ... in the American Revolution. Retrieved from Jstor.org: https://daily.jstor.org/intervention-american-revolution/.

overconfidence and a belief in its invincibility. This viewpoint suggests that neglecting to engage with potential allies diplomatically and underestimating the resolve of colonial dissent was born from hubris. Other scholars argue that Britain's aggressive stance was a calculated risk, part of a larger realpolitik strategy to quash potential rivals and consolidate power within key colonial holdings. Whatever the reasons, Great Britain cooked a stew of international resentment it was ultimately forced to eat.

The American allies required Great Britain to fight a war it did not want. The French alliance, forged in the crucible of mutual contempt for British domination, resulted in crucial military support for the American forces. With Spain's entry into the conflict, the theater of war expanded to the Mediterranean and the Spanish Main (the parts of the Spanish Empire in the Americas). The Dutch Republic's financial support and its nuanced approach to sustaining the American cause meant that Great Britain faced not just a military juggernaut but also a formidable financial adversary. Matters got progressively worse.

<u>The Native Americans</u>

In studies of the American Revolution, something that often escapes the limelight is the involvement of various Native American tribes. Their allegiances and actions paint complex patterns that influenced the trajectory of this historic conflict.

The indigenous landscape was a checkerboard of allegiances. The Oneida and Tuscarora stood with the fledgling United States, while the Mohawk, Seneca, Cayuga, and Onondaga sided with the British. Likewise, the Muscogee Nation and the Cherokee sided with the British, aiming to check American expansion into their lands.

British promises of honoring native land claims and preserving their way of life were not just rhetoric. Proclamations and treaties sought to secure Native American loyalty with perceived guarantees, although these promises often went unfulfilled. The line between genuine support and strategic manipulation by the British was thin, with Native Americans bearing the brunt of a revolution not of their making.

The Indian Confederacy, a union of various Native American nations, proved to be a malleable yet formidable supplement to British military efforts. Envisioned by British Superintendent of Indian Affairs Sir Guy Johnson and Mohawk leader Joseph Brant, the coalition was a shrewd diplomatic move that sidestepped the burgeoning movement for native sovereignty by leveraging inter-tribal tensions.

The alliance presented an opportunity for both parties. The British, by and large, saw in the confederacy a disruptive force to American expansion and a dependable military ally. For the Native Americans, it was a buffer against encroachment on their lands and a chance to reclaim territories and rights.[56]

Fracturing the Iroquois Nation

Once a powerful and unified confederacy, the American Revolution brought fissures within the Iroquois. Thayendanegea, also known as Joseph Brant, saw an opportune moment to harness British strength to help the Iroquois, leading many of his people to fight for the Crown. His sister, Molly Brant, worked parallel channels, securing Mohawk aid for the British cause.

As a statesman, warrior, and visionary, Brant was a formidable figure. He led devastating raids against American settlements, with his guerilla tactics earning him the moniker "Monster Brant" in American folklore. Brant was not without his detractors within the Mohawk community, and his decision to side with the British left a lingering legacy of resentment and displacement. He was a man of ambition, intent on securing the Mohawks' future in an ever-changing world.

The decision to side with the Americans was strategic and ideological for the Oneida and the Tuscarora. Led by Han Yerry, known as the Cherry Valley leader, these two tribes remained steadfast in their support.

The resulting split within the Iroquois Confederacy was more than just a rift; it was a fracture that would leave lasting scars, as brother fought brother in a bitter civil war.

Cherry Valley Massacre

The Cherry Valley massacre stands as an unforgettable testament to the confluence of agendas that converged to fuel the revolutionary era. Occurring on November 11th, 1778, in a small settlement in New York, the onslaught orchestrated by loyalist and indigenous forces sent shockwaves through the colonies.

---

[56] Makos, I. (2021, April 13). Roles of Native Americans during the American Revolution. Retrieved from Battlefields.org: https://www.battlefields.org/learn/articles/roles-native-americans-during-revolution.

The attack was a strategic endeavor to disrupt American expansion and cast doubt on the allure of independence. The brutality of the assault—a storm of flames and bullets that consumed the lives of patriots and civilians alike—served as a linchpin for the British strategy that saw in the Native Americans a potent weapon to counter the nascent Republic.

A campaign of retribution led by Generals James Clinton and John Sullivan followed. The mission was two-fold: to quench the Native American resistance and to displace them from lands they perceived as strategic barriers to American westward expansion.

The Clinton-Sullivan campaign, which commenced in 1779, sowed the seeds of a bitter harvest. As the American forces carved a path of destruction through the heart of Iroquois territory, they executed a scorched earth policy, decimating villages, crops, and resources vital for the sustenance and economic viability of the Native American nations. The campaign, therefore, was not simply a military expedition but also an act of aggression. The deliberate destruction of homesteads fractured social structures and uprooted the fabric of daily life. The Clinton-Sullivan campaign was a disaster from which the Iroquois Confederacy never fully recovered.[57]

The Tory Fifth Column

While battles were raging in the countryside, a civil war was waged within America that pitted the patriots, supporters of the evolution, against the Tories, supporters of the British Crown.

Tories, also known as loyalists, were American colonists loyal to the British monarchy during the revolutionary era. Their numbers, and therefore their impact, were significant. It is estimated that between 15 and 20 percent of the white population identified as loyalists—a substantial portion of colonial society. They included many prominent figures like the Anglican Church clergy and wealthy merchants with ties to Britain. Crown supporters included notable people, such as William Franklin, the royal governor of New Jersey and Benjamin Franklin's son. Their motivations ranged from a sense of patriotism for Britain to a fear of the unknown surrounding the patriot cause.

Tory numbers varied across the Thirteen Colonies, but they were mainly concentrated in the Middle Colonies, especially New York and

---

[57] National Park Service. (2024, February 18). The Clinton-Sullivan Campaign of 1779. Retrieved from Nps.gov: https://www.nps.gov/articles/000/the-clinton-sullivan-campaign-of-1779.htm.

Pennsylvania, which accounted for nearly half of the population. Other areas with large loyalist populations included the southern backcountry and coastal cities, such as Charleston and Wilmington.

Their allegiance to Britain was more than a simple proclamation; it also resulted in active service in British military units against the patriots, passive resistance, and outright sabotage of the revolution's cause. Tories were involved in some of the most infamous acts of the war, including the hanging of patriot prisoners, acting as guides for British forces during campaigns, and, in some cases, participating in atrocities, such as the Cherry Valley massacre, which saw the slaughter and displacement of patriot families.

Many Tories could not envision a world order without the British Empire at its center, believing firmly in the monarchy system. Some saw the rebellion as an affront to the social order and a step toward anarchy. Others feared the economic ramifications of severing ties with the British trade network.

For many loyalists who had built lives and identities rooted in their devotion to Great Britain, the prospect of an independent America threatened their sense of self and stability. They foresaw the complexities of creating a new government and were distrustful or skeptical of the promises and capabilities of the patriot leadership. Moreover, loyalists contended with the personal implications of losing their status, relationships, and livelihoods should the Crown fail to maintain control. Their resistance to independence was not born solely out of loyalty to the monarchy but also from a place of deep concern for the future of their families.

The loyalists were the subject of reprisals by the patriots, leading to a vicious cycle of violence and retribution that afflicted civilians on both sides of the conflict. These acts of violence against loyalists were part of a deliberate campaign to intimidate them from supporting the British.

African American Tories

The narrative of African Americans' involvement in this pivotal era often takes a backseat in historical accounts. Most are familiar with the story of Crispus Attucks and his role in the Boston Massacre.[58] What is

---

[58] For those who are not familiar with his story, Attucks was a sailor of mixed African and indigenous ancestry. He is regarded as the first person to die in the Boston Massacre. Some see him as the first American to be killed during the American Revolution.

less commonly shared but just as profound in its impact is the tale of the African American Tories. They were as much a part of the conflict as those who helped the patriots.

The Earl of Dunmore's Proclamation of 1775 represented a turning point for enslaved African Americans in the colonies. This controversial document promised freedom to any slave of a patriot who left their master and fought on the side of the British. What is not commonly known is that the earl of Dunmore owned slaves and that any runaways who were owned by loyalists were returned to their masters. The proclamation was not an emancipation but a reasonably successful recruiting scheme.

Approximately twenty thousand African Americans fought for the British in the American Revolution. Fighting units were created from the runaways. The Ethiopian Regiment, also known as Lord Dunmore's Ethiopian Regiment, was comprised of black slaves who joined the British. Other African Americans served in various units of the British army, including the Black Pioneers.

There were more than six hundred African Americans in the British ranks during the siege of Savannah in 1779. Dozens more served in support roles as cooks, guides, and laborers.[59]

It is estimated that five thousand African Americans fought for the patriot cause, notably the 1st Rhode Island Regiment.

It is essential to think about the motives and experiences of those who fought on either side. Patriotism or loyalty to the Crown were probably less important to these soldiers. Personal liberty and the chance to lead a better life would have been their primary motivations.

Saratoga was a turning point in the war, but it didn't mean the conflict would soon end. British command changed hands in 1778, and new British strategies were developed. The most brutal fighting of the American Revolution was in the years ahead.

---

[59] Mobley, C. (2006, September 24). Hundreds of African-Americans Campaigned for the King during 1779 Struggle for Savannah. Retrieved from Savannahnow.com: https://www.savannahnow.com/story/news/2006/09/25/hundreds-african-americans-campaigned-king-during-1779-struggle-savannah/13826035007/.

Chapter 9: Trying Times

John Burgoyne accused William Howe of sabotaging the Saratoga Campaign by not moving aggressively north to Albany. There might have been some personal animosity between the two, but Howe had a bigger prize in mind that, if won, would eclipse any success of Burgoyne.

The prize to be seized was Philadelphia, the rebel capital. Howe would lead an army of eighteen thousand men up the Chesapeake Bay, outflanking General George Washington's force that was in the rebel capital. Howe's capture of Philadelphia could be the masterstroke that would end the revolt. If Burgoyne successfully took Albany, that would be the icing on Howe's cake.

General Howe began his southern drive from New York City in late June. With an army of eighteen thousand men, Howe decided against a direct assault on Washington's entrenched forces and launched a maritime campaign to capture Philadelphia instead. His first objective was to navigate around Washington's army and cross New Jersey to reach the head of the Chesapeake Bay.

Washington's Preparations

George Washington was not idle; he was preparing for the arrival of the British. However, military preparations in the face of Howe's impending campaign were an immense task. Washington, whose army was still a fledgling force compared to the seasoned redcoats, sought to gather his troops and augment their numbers. Washington's meticulous preparation involved amassing men and morale; he was aware that the strength of his army lay not just in numbers but also in the tenacity and spirit of its individuals.

One of the most storied aspects of Washington's preparations was the fortification of the Delaware River, a strategic bulwark against Howe's anticipated advance. The construction of Fort Mifflin, a formidable structure on the river's edge, and the lesser-known works at Red Bank provide a glimpse into the labor-intensive enterprise aimed at stalling the British onslaught.

Engagement at Brandywine

Howe deftly employed flanking maneuvers, amphibious assaults, and practical subterfuge to outwit Washington's less disciplined troops. The rolling hills and dense forests provided ample cover for both the attackers and defenders. It also hindered communication and coordination—a dual-edged sword that would cut both ways.

The British advance was methodical, but it was contested. American resistance, guerrilla tactics, and a strategic decision not to engage in pitched battles unduly stretched the British supply lines and resolve. General Howe's route to Philadelphia might have been sprinkled with tactical victories, but it also bred strategic indecision that foreshadowed future repercussions.

The two armies met at Brandywine Creek on September 11th, 1777, each having fifteen thousand soldiers. Howe ordered General Wilhelm von Knyphausen to demonstrate against the Americans at Chadds Ford to distract them. At the same time, the main British force crossed the creek upstream. Howe's forces appeared on Washington's right flank, and von Knyphausen stuck hard.

The ferocity of the battle was only eclipsed by its scale. British soldiers, whose discipline was sharpened by the empire's many military campaigns, advanced with a precision that cut through the Continental lines. The Americans, with their characteristic bravery, fought fiercely. Washington's line eventually broke, but the Continental Army retreated in good order thanks to the rearguard defense of troops under Nathanael Greene. The road was open to Philadelphia for the British.[60]

In the face of the British advance, Washington faced the daunting prospect of defending a city against an enemy with naval superiority. He had to consider tactical maneuvers and the larger strategic picture. The

---

[60] Battlefields.org. (2024, February 21). Brandywine. Retrieved from Battlefields.org: https://www.battlefields.org/learn/revolutionary-war/battles/brandywine.

American commander decided to evacuate the capital, and the British entered Philadelphia on September 26th, 1777.

Washington's decision to abandon the city did not come lightly. It was a calculated move weighed against the prospect of a protracted and potentially debilitating siege. He was under no illusion about the symbolic and material loss of the colonial capital. His overarching concern was to preserve the Continental Army and, by extension, the revolution itself.

Battle of Germantown

General Howe wanted to capture the American fortifications on the Delaware River. He stationed nine thousand men under Generals James Grant and von Knyphausen in Germantown to protect Philadelphia. Desperate to regain the initiative, Washington gambled and attacked Germantown, hoping to score a success similar to the one gained at Trenton. He divided his forces between General John Sullivan and General Nathanael Greene and attacked the British on October 4th. A combination of the two groups being separated and Sullivan's men running out of ammunition created confusion and an opportunity for the British. The Americans were eventually forced to retreat.[61]

The engagement might have been a strategic loss since it did not impede the British occupation of Philadelphia. However, the significance of Germantown lies in its portrayal of American resolve. It showed that despite setbacks and inexperience, the colonists were willing and able to engage the British forces on their own terms.

Geopolitics Takes Center Stage

The autumn of 1777 should have been a splendid season for General William Howe. His campaign against Washington had been a great success, and the rebel capital was taken. Everything seemed wonderful, but disaster struck on October 17th when General Burgoyne surrendered his army.

The diplomatic fallout of Saratoga was no less severe. The surrender of Burgoyne's army was a significant victory for the American cause, reverberating across the Atlantic and shifting people's opinions in Europe. Most notably, the French, who had been covertly aiding the Americans, now openly sided with their cause, dramatically altering the

---

[61] Battlefields.org. (2024, February 21). Germantown. Retrieved from Battlefields.org: https://www.battlefields.org/learn/revolutionary-war/battles/germantown.

conflict's nature.

Moreover, the French were impressed with the colonists' conduct at Brandywine and Germantown. The Continental Army, though suffering defeats, remained resolute, showing adaptability and a commitment to the fight. Meanwhile, the British forces, though overwhelmingly powerful, struggled to translate that power into gaining a strategic advantage. The Americans were beaten but retreated in good order; they were not a disorganized mob.

Analysis of the Philadelphia Campaign

The failure of the British to deliver a knockout blow in the Philadelphia campaign had consequences that echoed far beyond the battlefield. The British victory did not bring a swift end to the rebellion: Washington's army remained intact and continued to harass Howe's army in a series of hit-and-run skirmishes, demonstrating the tenacity and determination of the American forces. Additionally, the British were now extended deep into hostile territory, which exposed their supply lines to constant attacks from colonial militias.

The inability of the British to maintain control over the newly captured territory left them increasingly isolated in Philadelphia. This isolation, combined with the demonstrated resolve of the American forces, began to sow seeds of doubt among the British leadership about the wisdom of continuing the war.

The decision to march on Philadelphia can be seen as a high-stakes gamble that failed to pay dividends for the British. Although they eventually captured the city, the cost of time and resources was significant. Their failure to fully capitalize on this victory and the subsequent strategic miscalculations that followed set the stage for the ultimate failure of British efforts in the American Revolution.

The Miracle of Valley Forge

The campaigning season ended, and the Continental Army moved to Valley Forge to quarter for the winter. They had been beaten by the British, but the Americans were still a fighting force. The Continental Army entered Valley Forge on December 17th, 1777, with approximately twelve thousand soldiers.

The winter at Valley Forge has since emerged as a potent symbol of endurance, suffering, and, ultimately, triumph in the annals of the American Revolutionary War. Narratives of resilience and sacrifice color this pivotal chapter in American history, as General George Washington and his Continental Army endured a brutal winter of disease, starvation, and harsh living conditions. The conventional tale of Valley Forge conjures images of ragged soldiers, frostbitten feet, and a beleaguered commander in chief grappling with a struggle against the British Empire.

The Continental Army arrived at Valley Forge following several defeats and retreats. The soldiers wore ragged clothing and suffered from widespread hunger. Many did not even have shoes to protect them from the snow. The winter claimed the lives of nearly 2,500 soldiers due to various hardships, but the suffering extended beyond mere physical deprivation.

The army was demoralized, and discipline was waning. The men faced an enemy that had occupied the capital and a hostile winter landscape. Washington's challenge was to keep his men alive, sustain the revolutionary fervor, and command an effective fighting force against the superior British military might come spring. The logistics of supplying and supporting his forces seemed impossible; it was a test of both his leadership and the will to win.

The First Days

The topography of Valley Forge and the harsh winter provided a natural challenge, but a lack of provisions and poor planning exacerbated the situation. Troops were exposed to the elements with inadequate clothing, shelter, and food. Frostbite was widespread, and many went hungry. Disease, particularly smallpox, was rampant in the close quarters of the encampment. It seemed as if the suffering was ceaseless. The very survival of the Continental Army was in question.[62]

---

[62] Keesling, D. K. (2024, February 21). Valley Forge: A Place of Transformation for the Continental Army. Retrieved from Thepursuitofhistory.org: https://thepursuitofhistory.org/2022/10/24/valley-forge-a-place-of-transformation-for-the-continental-army/.

Soldiers' quarters at Valley Forge.
Dr. Blazer, CC BY-SA 4.0 <https://creativecommons.org/licenses/by-sa/4.0>, via Wikimedia Commons; https://commons.wikimedia.org/wiki/File:Soldier%27s_Quarters_at_Valley_Forge.jpg

Thomas Paine's *The American Crisis*, a series of pamphlets published throughout the war, provided the intellectual ammunition for the soldiers' morale. His words, "These are the times that try men's souls," served as a clarion call for perseverance and resistance.[63] Paine's works transcended the written page, becoming a rallying cry that resonated within the hearts of every soldier at Valley Forge.

Washington had more to worry about than just his troops' physical distress and morale. His leadership was being seriously questioned.

The Conway Cabal

The problems started before the troops arrived at Valley Forge. The Conway Cabal was a conspiracy of ambitious people who were highly critical of George Washington and wanted him removed as commander of the Continental Army. The primary conspirator was Thomas Conway, an Irish-French soldier known for his intelligence and gallantry. Conway was also fiercely critical of Washington's military leadership, and he was not alone. Horatio Gates, the hero of Saratoga, aligned with Conway to

---

[63] Paine, T. (1776). The American Crisis. Retrieved from Library of Congress: https://www.loc.gov/resource/cph.3b06889/.

91

question Washington's position. Congressman Thomas Mifflin and, allegedly, Benjamin Rush also disapproved of Washington's leadership. Their grievances against the commander in chief ranged from handling military campaigns to personal disagreements.

A flurry of correspondence with questions about Washington's competence ensued. Washington was informed about it and received Conway, who was promoted to inspector general by the Continental Congress, with cold courtesy when Conway visited Valley Forge in late December. Washington's professional demeanor caused Conway to back down, and he wrote a letter of apology to Washington. The plot fizzled as more about the conspiracy became public. Attempts to orchestrate a "no confidence" vote in Washington were fiercely disputed in Congress. The final consequence of the Conway Cabal was that it consolidated Washington's standing as a unifying symbol of American resilience and resolve.[64]

The Drill Officer

General Washington's leadership during this time was crucial. The soldiers needed to become more professional to have a chance against the British in the coming year. At Washington's request, officers taught the soldiers European military tactics and instilled discipline, marking a turning point in the Continental Army's professionalism. The arrival in the camp of a unique individual enhanced their training.

This man's name was Friedrich Wilhelm von Steuben, and he claimed to be a baron and a former lieutenant general of the Prussian Army (Washington later discovered that von Steuben was no more than a captain who was born a commoner). Von Steuben was highly recommended by Benjamin Franklin and proved to be a superior military trainer.

[64] Scythes, J. (2024, February 21). Conway Cabal. Retrieved from Mountvernon.org: https://www.mountvernon.org/library/digitalhistory/digital-encyclopedia/article/conway-cabal/#:~:text=The%20Conway%20Cabal%20refers%20to,with%20Major%20General%20Horatio%20Gates.

Portrait of von Steuben.
https://commons.wikimedia.org/wiki/File:Baron_Steuben_by_Peale,_1780.jpg

Von Steuben's purpose was simple yet profound: he was to instill discipline and tactics in the Continental Army, which were hitherto nonexistent, transforming it from a loose coalition of militias into a unified fighting force. His approach was rigorous and methodical. He drilled the soldiers in the art of war, from basic maneuvers to complex formations that would be essential on the battlefield. His "Blue Book," a training manual that would become the cornerstone of American military education, standardized the army's techniques and military protocol.

Von Steuben's contributions transcended the tactical; he reformed the army's administrative systems, established rigorous standards of hygiene and health management, and integrated training for soldiers of all ethnicities and languages in an act of profound inclusivity. The unity forged in the fires of adversity kindled a new spirit among the troops.[65]

---

[65] Mary Stockwell, P. (2024, February 21). Baron Von Steuben. Retrieved from Mountvernon.org: https://www.mountvernon.org/library/digitalhistory/digital-encyclopedia/article/baron-von-steuben/.

His efforts generated results. The soldiers emerged from Valley Forge as a cohesive unit and as seasoned combatants. The transformation was remarkable; what was once a dispirited band was now a source of pride, a force bedecked with a newfound sense of discipline and confidence. Von Steuben's training had forged soldiers and stewards of a new nation's future. Washington was ready to take on the British and fight on a level playing field.

At the heart of the Valley Forge narrative is the leadership of George Washington.

Washington's advocacy for his soldiers, his willingness to share their suffering, and his unyielding belief in their ability to triumph against all odds forged a bond of trust between leader and army. This trust and the resilience nurtured within the encampment formed the backbone of the American military ethos.

<u>1778 Military Strategy</u>

Washington and his advisors devised a multi-faceted campaign to cement alliances with European powers while maintaining pressure on British troops. The campaign's goals included the following:

- Consolidating military presence: Expanding control over crucial areas to enhance the Continental Army's strategic position.
- International diplomacy: Leveraging military successes to garner support from France and other potential European allies.
- Domestic morale boost: Building on earlier victories to reinforce the the revolutionary spirit among the populace and the troops.

These objectives underpinned a series of maneuvers that combined military prowess with a statesman's eye for global politics.

One of the most significant facets of the campaign of 1778 was the successful negotiation of the Franco-American alliance, which was formalized on February 6th, 1778. French support was a game changer, as the French brought a formidable naval force that could challenge British maritime dominance. The Treaty of Alliance solidified the collaboration, which promised mutual military assistance against the British.[66]

[66] Encyclopedia.com. (2024, January 30). Franco-American Alliance. Retrieved from Britannica.com: https://www.britannica.com/event/Franco-American-Alliance.

Sir Henry Clinton

William Howe resigned as the commander in chief of the British army in North America when he learned of Burgoyne's defeat. He remained in Philadelphia until May 24th, 1778, and was replaced by Sir Henry Clinton.

Machiavelli's political treatise, *The Prince*, advocates for practicality over ethics, a philosophy that often shapes the approach of political and military leaders. Clinton embodied this pragmatism in his strategic decisions as he sought a path to victory filled with tactical caution and calculated risks. His mission was to wage war and win it by any means necessary.

Clinton believed the British army needed a place and some time to regroup and reorganize to succeed. He decided New York was the place to do both. To him, Philadelphia had no strategic value. Consequently, on June 18th, 1778, Clinton and fifteen thousand British troops evacuated Philadelphia, leaving the loyalists behind in panic for their lives.[67]

Battle of Monmouth

General George Washington led the Continental Army to strike a blow against the British forces retreating from Philadelphia. The campaign was marked by tactical retreats, scorched earth policies, and the cloak-and-dagger strategies of spying and intelligence gathering.

The Battle of Monmouth, fought on June 28th, 1778, was significant for several reasons. It was one of the most extensive engagements of the war, involving over twenty-six thousand soldiers. The intense heat of the day and a lack of proper decision-making—most notably, the controversial performance of Major General Charles Lee, who ordered a retreat that enabled a British counterattack—contributed to a battle that culminated in a draw. The British ultimately moved on to New York City but not without suffering heavy casualties.

The resolve and resilience displayed by the soldiers who braved the blistering heat and the chaos of the battle instilled a newfound confidence within the ranks. The stories of men's courage and sacrifice spread, kindling the embers of hope and determination. Monmouth demonstrated the growing proficiency of the Continental Army. This performance galvanized public opinion in favor of the patriot cause and

---

[67] Editors, H. (2024, February 21). British Abandon Philadelphia. Retrieved from History.com: https://www.history.com/this-day-in-history/british-abandon-philadelphia.

dispelled any lingering doubts about the viability of the American forces.

The new British commander in chief was in a peculiar position. Great Britain had overwhelming military might, better funding, and a robust navy controlling critical waterways. However, an extended supply chain and a growing aversion to the war within Britain demanded an expedited resolution. Moreover, the Continental Army was proving resilient. Henry Clinton decided on a change of direction.[68]

His solution was in the South, a theater of war that was less populated and less defended. His strategy centered on a belief that by securing the South, British control over the colonies might crumble the rebellion. This Southern Campaign, as it was dubbed, was a concerted effort to exploit divisions within the American leadership and populace. The bloodiest days of the American Revolution were about to begin.

[68] National Park Service. (2024, February 21). Henry Clinton. Retrieved from Nps.gov: https://www.nps.gov/people/henry-clinton.htm#:~:text=Sir%20Henry%20Clinton%20replaced%20Sir,to%20face%20the%20rebellious%20American .

Chapter 10: The Southern Campaign

The more well-known conflicts in the North often overshadow the battles of the Southern Campaign. Yet, these engagements were vital in the larger strategy of both the Continental Army and the British forces. Here, the loyalists, colloquially referred to as Tories, formed a significant force that defended British interests and shaped the course of the American Revolutionary War. The decision to remain loyal was often complex, influenced by socioeconomic status, cultural ties, and the belief that British governance offered greater stability. Thomas Brown, Patrick Ferguson, and David Fanning were instrumental in leading loyalist militia units. These leaders were skilled tacticians and adept at cultivating support from local loyalists, often by suppressing patriot activities.

Loyalists saw the conflict through the lens of law and order, with a deep distrust of what they viewed as the anarchy inherent in the patriot movement. Their loyalty was often rooted in a conservative worldview that prized stability and tradition over the revolutionary fervor gripping the patriots.

The Reliance on Loyalists

The loyalist population in the south was sizeable but less uniform in its support for the British than the British thought. Amidst the conflicting loyalties and complex social dynamics, many aspired to remain neutral, forsaking the British and the colonial militias. These allegiances were often fluid, influenced by immediate circumstances and the local progress of the war.

The military presence of the British and their loyalist allies emboldened some to declare their support openly, igniting a bitter civil war within the revolutionary movement. It is estimated that around 20 percent of white southern colonists were Tory loyalists, with a notable concentration in South Carolina and Georgia. The British sought to utilize this population to create a political and military base.

The Georgia Phase

The Southern Campaign began with a foray into the most southern colony, Georgia. This was the last American colony settled by Great Britain, so Clinton assumed the Georgians would welcome the presence of British soldiers to defend the civilians against Native Americans.

On November 26th, 1778, Clinton sent nearly three thousand soldiers under Lieutenant Colonel Archibald Campbell to Savannah with instructions to take the city. Savannah's defenses included swampy land that the patriots believed would prevent a British advance. However, a slave pointed out an undefended trail that led to the Continental Army's barracks. A strong detachment of British soldiers followed that path and effectively flanked the Americans.

Savannah fell on December 29th, 1778. A significant number of American soldiers were taken prisoner. Loyalists aided the British in taking Savannah, and that was the start of an alliance that would be highly successful in the coming months.

Savannah was now a base of operations for the British. Augusta would later fall as British and Tory forces began raiding into South Carolina. Georgia would formally receive a royal governor in July 1779. A later effort to retake the city by a combined American and French force resulted in a failed siege that lasted from September 16th to October 20th, 1779.[69]

There were American victories at Port Royal Island, South Carolina, and at Kettle Creek, Georgia. The backcountry of Georgia was still in American hands, but the situation became dramatically worse in late December 1779. Sir Henry Clinton sailed from New York City with fourteen thousand men to Charleston, South Carolina, to besiege that significant southern port.

[69] Battlefields.org. (2024, February 20). Siege of Savannah. Retrieved from Battlefields.org: https://www.battlefields.org/learn/revolutionary-war/battles/savannah.

The Fall of Charleston

The siege of Charleston began in earnest on April 1st, 1780. It lasted until May 12th, when ill-equipped American forces commanded by General Benjamin Lincoln surrendered Charleston to British troops under General Sir Henry Clinton. The swift and decisive blow dealt to the patriot forces spelled the largest surrender of American troops until World War II, with over 5,500 soldiers laying down their arms.

The siege was a flagrant display of British military might. In the broader narrative, one can infer the beginning of the end for the revolutionary cause in the southern theater. The loyalists in Charleston benefited tremendously from this British victory.

A depiction of the siege of Charleston.
https://commons.wikimedia.org/wiki/File:Sullivans-island-1050x777.jpg

The Loyalist Opposition

The population of Charleston was significantly divided. While patriots fervently rallied for independence, a distinct and substantial segment of the population remained loyalist, with notables such as Rawlins Lowndes staunchly advocating for the Crown.

The political and cultural divisions were most pronounced in the South Carolinian socioeconomic elite. Due to longstanding trade connections and familial ties to England, these individuals became a bridge—albeit a delicate one—between the burgeoning American identity and European heritage.

The siege of Charleston cast a long shadow. For the loyalists, the British capture of Charleston was a moment of victory and presented them with a terrible risk. Their fortunes and their lives depended on British success. Failure would leave the loyalists in the hands of a patriot faction looking for revenge.

The Collapse of South Carolina

Following the capture of Charleston, the British military embarked on a series of armed conflicts designed to assert their supremacy and discourage rebellion. Some of the most prominent among these clashes were the Battle of Waxhaws and the Battle of Camden.

The Battle of Waxhaws pitted the Americans under Abraham Buford against Banastre Tarleton on May 29th, 1780. This was a small battle, but the aftermath was shocking. Americans who were trying to surrender were massacred by British soldiers surging through the broken American lines, generating the phrase "Tarleton's quarter" as a description of British barbarity. By the summer of 1780, the American revolutionaries had begun to feel the weight of British resurgence under the command of General Charles Cornwallis.

The Battle of Camden happened on August 16th, 1780. The British were commanded by General Cornwallis. Horatio Gates, the hero of Saratoga, led the Americans. The nature of the battle was asymmetrical, with the well-drilled ranks of the British pitted against the Americans. The British numbered around 2,200, while the American force tallied approximately 3,700. Strategies from both sides aimed to exploit each other's weaknesses, with Cornwallis seeking to assert British dominance in the South through a swift and decisive victory and Gates hoping to bolster American morale with a successful defense.[70]

The Battle of Camden was a disaster for the Americans. In the face of a relentless British advance, the American lines crumbled, and the troops from Virginia fled, leaving the Continental Army exposed. Troops under Johann de Kalb stayed on the field as other Americans ran for their lives. The casualty count was devasting, and de Kalb was killed. The reputation of General Gates was destroyed, as the American

---

[70] Battlefields.org. (2024, February 20). Waxhaws. Retrieved from Battlefields.org: https://www.battlefields.org/learn/revolutionary-war/battles/waxhaws.

commander fled the field and did not stop running until he had covered more than 150 miles.[71]

Organized American resistance was eliminated at Camden. Only disorganized militiamen and guerrillas were left to fight the British troops and their Tory allies. It would take an aggressive commander to save the revolutionary cause in the South. That miracle worker was a Quaker from Rhode Island.

Nathanael Greene and His Strategy

Nathanael Greene was one of the most capable and audacious generals of the American Revolutionary War. He was born into a devout Quaker family in Rhode Island in 1742. Unlike the dogmatic pacifism of his upbringing, Greene was drawn to the intellectual ferment that gave rise to the revolutionary cause. His military acumen quickly elevated him through the ranks when the conflict erupted.

He was one of the most innovative and strategic minds of his time, known for his tactical flexibility, logistical acumen, and ability to inspire troops. Greene's strategic vision considered the constraints of massive distances, poor roads, and the growing state of the Continental Army. His approach to warfare was innovative at a time when the conventional wisdom of European military orthodoxy held sway.

In 1780, Greene was appointed as commander of the Southern Department, facing an almost impossible situation. The British had just captured Charleston, and British General Cornwallis seemed unstoppable. Greene, however, refused to accept defeat. His strategy was to relentlessly harry the British, wearing down their forces through attrition and quick, carefully chosen battles that capitalized on American advantages.

[71] Battlefields.org. (2024, February 20). Camden. Retrieved from Battlefields.org: https://www.battlefields.org/learn/revolutionary-war/battles/camden.

Portrait of Nathanael Greene.

Greene's Plan for Victory

Morale among American forces had plummeted, and the economic and social fabric of the South was in dire straits. Greene faced a deceptively simple yet daunting task: to rally a demoralized army and turn the tide of war against the formidable British presence.

With compassion and a sharp understanding of human nature, Greene embarked on a twofold mission to rejuvenate his forces. He recognized that victory on the battlefield was but one facet of the war; resilience and resolve were equally crucial. Greene restored confidence through relentless training, instilling discipline and fostering unity among the disparate militia groups that comprised the southern army. His leadership style eschewed authoritarianism in favor of a participatory approach, earning him the respect and loyalty of his men.

Aware that conventional tactics would fail to redress the imbalance, Greene embraced unorthodox methods to outmaneuver the superior British forces. He repeatedly withdrew his army, utilizing the South's expansive geography to his advantage. His knowledge of the local terrain allowed him to play to the strengths of irregular warfare, leveraging the speed and stealth of his forces to harry the British without committing to head-on confrontations.

Moreover, Greene recognized the importance of maintaining the local population's support. He forbade his troops from engaging in the wanton destruction that often accompanied war, instead appealing to the southern civility ingrained in social structures. By winning over the hearts and minds of the people, Greene developed a network of intelligence and a continuous flow of recruits that sustained the patriot effort.

Fabian Strategy, Southern Style

What Greene was doing was similar to Washington's plan of action after the fall of New York City, but there was a difference. Greene's strategy was one of attrition, in which the goal was not to defeat the British outright but to wear down their will and resources. He effectively stretched the British supply lines through his tactical retreats, forcing them to overextend and weaken their grip on the southern territory. This relentless pressure, coupled with the irregular engagements that disproportionately taxed British forces, hastened the erosion of British strength.

At this time, a highly effective guerrilla leader was Francis Marion, who was also known as the "Swamp Fox." Operating in the swamps of South Carolina, Marion's irregular tactics became a thorn in the side of the British forces. His leadership of small bands of militia allowed for sudden strikes and rapid disappearances into the familiar marshlands, disrupting enemy communications, supply chains, and fortifications.

Francis Marion's unconventional warfare dovetailed with Greene's approach of avoiding large-scale engagements in favor of a war of attrition. He could strike swiftly and without warning, sapping British morale and helping regain control of the South Carolina backcountry. His actions not only weakened the British but also provided Greene with vital intelligence and preserved the fighting spirit of the patriot cause in the South.

Overmountain Men

In the frontier lands of Virginia, the Carolinas, and Tennessee, a group of rugged settlers known as the Overmountain Men began coalescing. These frontiersmen, primarily of Scottish-Irish descent, were fiercely independent. They had migrated to escape the authority of the coastal elites and carved out an existence in the wilderness. When the call to arms echoed through the mountains, the Overmountain Men saw an opportunity to strike a blow against the loyalists they despised. Despite the challenging obstacles of distance and terrain, they united under the command of several leaders, most notably Benjamin Cleveland, John Sevier, and William Campbell. They set out on a dangerous march to the Piedmont region of South Carolina to fight.

Major Patrick Ferguson, a British officer in command of the loyalist militia, opposed them. Known for his sharpshooting and discipline, Ferguson set his sights on hunting down patriots in the southern backcountry. His proclamation that he would " hang their leaders and lay their country waste "spurred the patriots into action. Ferguson's overconfidence and contempt for the patriots, whom he thought a "rabble" not worth pursuing, proved to be a fatal miscalculation.

A Fight on a Mountainside

The battle occurred on October 7th, 1780, at Kings Mountain, South Carolina. It began as an encirclement. The Overmountain Men, who had been preparing for combat during their march, used their knowledge of the mountainous terrain to their advantage. They attacked from all sides, moving in small groups, covering under the brush, and shouting, "Remember Waxhaws!" The loyalists, unprepared for this style of warfare, quickly found themselves surrounded and outflanked, their morale broken and their force divided.

In a heated and brutal fight that lasted barely an hour, the tide turned decisively in favor of the patriots. Ferguson was slain, and the loyalists, leaderless and outnumbered, suffered heavy casualties. The patriots secured a resounding victory, capturing more than a thousand prisoners, although the number is still a topic of historical debate and was initially exaggerated.

The Tory prisoners faced frontier justice. On October 14th, drumhead courts-martial were held, and thirty-six loyalists were convicted of various offenses. Nine were hanged before the proceedings were stopped. The remaining prisoners escaped or were paroled.[72]

The victory at Kings Mountain altered the trajectory of the war in the Carolinas. It marked the high point in patriot morale for a conflict that had, until that moment, been a series of setbacks and retreats. Kings Mountain energized the revolutionary cause in the South, ending the British presence in the western Carolinas.

The victory came at an opportune time. Nathanael Greene's troops were ready to engage the enemy.

Greene's Offensive

General Greene divided his forces, luring Cornwallis deeper into the hostile interior of the Carolinas. Greene's soldiers steadily chipped away at the British by leveraging local knowledge and utilizing hit-and-run tactics. His decision to avoid an open battle against a superior enemy was among the most challenging, but it ultimately paid off. The colonial forces, comprised of regulars and militia, gradually gained confidence as they inflicted casualties and captured supplies. The year 1781 witnessed several significant battles as the British and Americans fought to control the Carolinas.

- Cowpens

The Battle of Cowpens took place on January 17th, 1781. This battle stands out as a masterstroke of military strategy and demonstrated the effective use of coordinated ranks and militia forces under American commanders Brigadier General Daniel Morgan and Colonel Andrew Pickens.

On the rolling fields of the South Carolina upcountry, Morgan employed a tactical double envelopment that integrated the use of Continental Army regulars, militia fighters, and cavalry in a sophisticated retreat-and-counterattack maneuver. The American forces effectively lured the British into a false sense of victory as the frontline militia performed a planned retreat, only for the British to be met by a staunch line of Continental Army regulars who withstood the British charge and fought back with ferocity. The British forces, led by Banastre Tarleton, were decisively defeated, suffering heavy casualties. The British loss significantly contributed to the weakening of British military operations in the southern colonies.

---

[72] Revolutionarywar.us. (2024, February 21). The Battle of Kings Mountain. Retrieved from Revolutionarywar.us: https://revolutionarywar.us/year-1780/battle-kings-mountain/.

- Guilford Court House

On March 15th, the American and British forces met in the fields around Guilford Courthouse, North Carolina. The outcome was a tactical victory for the British, who held the field at the end of the day. Yet, it was a Pyrrhic victory. While Cornwallis technically won the battle, his forces were severely depleted. On the other hand, Americans held their ground and did not suffer the catastrophic losses of Camden. Greene and his men withdrew, leaving the British in control of the battlefield but without the tactical advantage they had gained from previous encounters. Cornwallis retreated to Wilmington, North Carolina, for reinforcements and supplies.

- Siege of Ninety-Six

The siege of Ninety-six took place ninety-six miles from the nearest Cherokee village; the town was a major crossroads in western South Carolina. Greene laid siege to the Star Fort located there and its loyalist garrison from May 22nd to June 18th. He broke the siege when he learned a relief force was coming from Charleston.

Cornwallis Abandons the Carolinas

Cornwallis's struggle to assert British control in the Carolinas brought him face to face with the realities of the southern conflict: a lack of popular support, logistical difficulties, and an adaptable, if not always conventional, American response. The Southern Campaign was costly in terms of lives and resources, which the delicate British supply lines struggled to maintain. The specter of French and Spanish intervention in the war loomed over military decision-making, already complicating matters elsewhere.

The global context of the war meant that, for the British, maintaining a presence in the already secured southern territories had to be weighed against opportunities and threats elsewhere. Virginia, as one of the wealthier and more populous colonies, offered strategic advantages in recruiting loyalist fighters and supplies, and it represented a central location from which to launch operations in other theaters of the war.

Cornwallis recognized that Greene was being supplied from Virginia. The British general hoped to cut off the supply lines to Greene and proposed to Lord George Germain, Secretary of State for the Colonies, that he, Cornwallis, should invade Virginia. Germain ignored the chain of command, which would have meant that Sir Henry Clinton would be involved in the decision-making, and agreed to Cornwallis's idea.

Cornwallis then left Wilmington and headed north to Virginia with his army.[73]

Greene continued a mop-up campaign in the Carolinas, driving what was left of the British to Charleston and Wilmington. The Battle of Eutaw Springs on September 8th, 1781, was the last major battle in the Carolinas. The British were no longer able to stop Nathanael Greene.

Nathanael Greene's stewardship of the Southern Department was integral to the patriots' victory in the American Revolutionary War. Greene's legacy exemplifies how the underdog can prevail through cunning, adaptability, and courage.

Benedict Arnold's Treason

The story of Benedict Arnold is often cited as the ultimate tale of betrayal in American history. Once a celebrated and courageous military leader for the fledgling United States, Arnold's legacy was forever stained by his decision to become a turncoat and offer the strategic fort of West Point to the British during the American Revolutionary War. His name, once synonymous with selfless patriotism, metamorphosed into a benchmark for disloyalty. However, the motivations behind Arnold's betrayal and the intricate events leading up to his plan paint a complex picture of a man and a nation at the crossroads of history.

Before he became America's villain, Benedict Arnold was an ardent and courageous supporter of the American cause. He was renowned for his bravery during the Battles of Saratoga in 1777, where his tactical brilliance helped secure a critical victory for the Continental Army. Despite his achievements, Arnold felt a profound sense of betrayal by the government he had served so faithfully.

Disillusioned by the lack of recognition, compensation, and the promotion of other officers ahead of him, Arnold's disenchantment simmered. Simultaneously, personal slights and accusations of misconduct tarnished his reputation in the eyes of the American leadership. These grievances laid the groundwork for Arnold's eventual turn to the enemy.

Unbeknownst to Washington and other senior officers, Benedict Arnold was communicating secretly with Sir Henry Clinton. The American general knew he was being considered for the command of

---

[73] Revolutionarywar.us. (2024, February 21). Southern Theater. Retrieved from Revolutionarywar.us: https://revolutionarywar.us/campaigns/1775-1782-southern-theater/.

West Point. On July 12th, 1780, he sent a coded message to Clinton, offering to surrender West Point to the British once he was placed in command. The price for the treason was £20,000.

Situated on the Hudson River north of New York City, West Point carried immense military importance during the American Revolutionary War. Its control divided the northern and southern states, ensuring a critical line of defense against British advancement. West Point provided a secure base for the Continental Army to store arms and munitions. Arnold's plot to surrender West Point to the British was a potential coup that could have altered the war's course. His actions would have not only delivered a devastating blow to the Continental Army but also provided a morale boost for the British, who had been unable to make inroads in the face of colonial resistance.

Benedict Arnold became commander of West Point on August 3rd, 1780. He received a coded message from Clinton on August 15th, accepting Arnold's price for the fort. West Point would be a British outpost in a few days.

The Plot Revealed

Everything was going according to plan. However, Arnold's plot started to fall apart when his British contact, Major John André, was caught by the Americans on September 23rd. Papers containing incriminating evidence were found on the British officer, detailing the financial offers to Arnold for turning traitor and providing tangible proof of his collusion.

With the discovery of John André and the damning evidence in his possession, Arnold hastily fled West Point on September 24th. In the early morning hours, he boarded a waiting barge and insisted under the pretense of security that the crew row him down the Hudson River to the HMS *Vulture*, a British sloop of war. Through this daring escape, Arnold avoided capture by mere hours. George Washington arrived at West Point to find his disgraced general already gone.

Portrait of Benedict Arnold.
https://commons.wikimedia.org/wiki/File:Benedict_Arnold_1color.jpg

Upon joining the British ranks, he was commissioned as a brigadier general but received a lukewarm reception from his new peers, who viewed him with suspicion and never fully accepted him. Arnold led British forces in several raids, including an attack on New London, Connecticut, which was considered by many as a ruthless act against his compatriots. Despite these efforts, the rewards and recognition he had hoped to gain from the British were modest at best.

The discovery of Arnold's scheme was perhaps equally if not more critical than the intended treachery. Preventing the British occupation of West Point preserved the stronghold as a linchpin of American defense and bolstered the resolve and trust in each other within the revolutionary leadership. Benedict Arnold received lasting fame, but he is remembered as an infamous traitor, not a devoted patriot.

Chapter 11: Yorktown

<u>War on the Frontier</u>

One area we haven't looked at yet is the west. The land west of the Appalachians was fiercely contested. The vast lands comprising modern-day Ohio, Indiana, Illinois, Michigan, and Wisconsin were the battleground where small bands of patriots, Shawnee and Delaware warriors, and French settlers fought to repel British and loyalist incursions. The American Revolution on the frontier was a struggle for land and identity, and the tenuous alliance between settlers and indigenous peoples reshaped conflict dynamics.

The vast resources of the northwest—primarily furs, timber, and highly fertile land—made it an economic prize for any power that could secure it. The British created a formidable barrier to American westward expansion by controlling the fur trade and the Ohio River.

The establishment and conquest of forts were pivotal in controlling the vast territory west of the Appalachians. Fort Vincennes, Fort Kaskaskia, and other strongholds shifted several times between British and American hands, as both sides vied to control these strategic positions. Each skirmish was a calculated risk that would either extend the boundaries of American influence or reinforce British occupation.

<u>The Inhabitants</u>

The French presence in the northwest added a layer of complexity to the conflict. While French settlers had enjoyed relative autonomy and were wary of American expansion, they were equally discontent with British rule. Myriad loyalties and an overarching desire for self-governance characterized their role in the American Revolution.

American settlers played a pivotal role during the war. These frontiersmen carved out settlements in hostile landscapes, creating homes and communities in the face of untold hardships. Many settlers joined local militias or the Continental Army during the conflict, providing manpower in critical battles and campaigns. Their intimate knowledge of the frontier's rivers, forests, and mountains proved invaluable in countering British strategies, and their resilience in the face of adversity added a crucial layer to the colonial war effort.

Indigenous tribes were central figures in the western theater. They played a complex and often decisive role in the unfolding conflict. Native American nations like the Shawnee, Delaware, and Miami found themselves in a precarious position as they faced pressure from American colonists and British forces. While some tribes sought to remain neutral, others entered into alliances that they hoped would preserve their territories and way of life. As allies to the British, they contributed significantly to the defense of territories, using their knowledge of the land, guerrilla tactics, and strategic insight to stem the tide of American expansion.[74]

British Western Strategy

In the aftermath of the French and Indian War, the Royal Proclamation of 1763 was announced. To mitigate potential tensions with indigenous peoples and their alliances, the proclamation drew a demarcation line along the crest of the Appalachian Mountains, effectively preventing colonial expansion westward.

In theory, the proclamation sought to foster peaceful coexistence with the indigenous nations, who were now to be managed under the Crown's direct authority. The British were adept at the art of treaty-making and alliance-building, using a combination of coercion and promises to maintain a patchwork of alliances among the indigenous nations. They built a series of fortresses to secure their western territory.

These fortresses weren't just physical bulwarks; they were also a testament to Britain's commitment to holding the line against any potential colonial insurgency. Forts like Fort Niagara, Fort Toronto, and

[74] Orrison, R. (2024, January 3). Native American Impact on British War Strategy in Southern Campaign. Retrieved from Battlefields.org: https://www.battlefields.org/learn/articles/native-american-impact-british-war-strategy-southern-campaign.

Fort Detroit were built to assert British dominance, control strategic points, and keep indigenous nations on the side of the Crown. They also served as outposts for the fur trade.

American Goals and Objectives

The frontier represented an opportunity for untapped economic potential, with natural resources in abundance and land offering a fresh start. The motivation to venture west was a heady mix of economic opportunity, the pursuit of freedom, and a deep-rooted sense of Manifest Destiny.

The American patriots viewed the British presence in the western frontier as a barrier to their expansionist aspirations and a threat to their burgeoning national identity. British forts in the west served as a reminder of Britain's dominance, and British alliances with Native American tribes were seen as strategic moves to limit access to these lands and to stir up resistance against settler encroachment. Such actions by the British only fueled the colonists' resolve to push the frontier westward.

Military Campaigns on the Western Frontier

In 1779, Major General Frederick Haldimand, the commanding officer in the British Province of Quebec, directed a formidable expedition under Lieutenant Colonel Henry Bird. Bird's forces, composed of British regulars, loyalists, and Native American allies, conducted swift and devastating attacks on American settlements in the western frontiers of Virginia and Pennsylvania. The British sought to resurrect the dispirit of the loyalist citizenry while safeguarding the lucrative fur trade against American encroachments.

An equal measure of resilience and adaptability marked the American response to British incursions in the west. Leaders such as George Rogers Clark and Brigadier General Daniel Brodhead would become synonymous with the American campaign in the hinterland. Clark, a daring and resourceful frontiersman, embarked on a campaign that was instrumental in securing the vast expanse of the Illinois Country for the American cause. His audacious march from the falls of the Ohio River to the strategic outposts of Kaskaskia and Cahokia showcased the reach of the patriots' territorial ambitions.

With a contingent of disciplined militiamen and frontiersmen, Clark captured British-held Fort Vincennes in a February 1779 siege. This strategic victory at Vincennes was pivotal; it weakened British influence in the region and delivered a profound psychological blow to their military posture. He demonstrated the capability of the irregular American forces to conduct significant operations in hostile territory.

The British redoubled their efforts to regain the upper hand, dispatching more troops and resources to fortify their remaining strongholds and repel the American advances. Lieutenant Governor Henry Hamilton, a key British figure in the region known as the "Hair Buyer" for reportedly incentivizing the scalping of rebels, was quick to act, reclaiming Fort Sackville at Vincennes.

Clark refused to accept this defeat. Instead, he mounted a counter-offensive in the winter of 1779. In an unexpected turn, he led a lean force of frontiersmen through the flooded plains of the Wabash River, laying siege once again to Fort Sackville. Clark's forces successfully recaptured the fort and took Hamilton prisoner in what would be remembered as one of the most audacious operations of the American Revolutionary War.[75]

A Continuing Stalemate

During the years 1780 and 1781, the military situation in the western frontier of the American Revolution became a complex stalemate characterized by sporadic skirmishes and strategic maneuvers rather than large-scale battles. The British forces maintained their presence in key strongholds, but their domination in the region was contested by American troops, who were well accustomed to the rigors of wilderness fighting.

In this period, the American forces aimed to solidify their hold on the Illinois Country, counteract British efforts to fortify their positions, and incite Native American aggression. A notable event came in August 1780 when Clark led the Kentucky militia in a retaliatory attack known as the August Expedition against the Shawnee towns along the Mad River, a response to Native Americans allied with the British.

Strained by extended supply lines and facing an enemy familiar with the territory, British forces struggled to execute a successful strategy. American troops, although fewer in number, utilized guerrilla tactics and their intimate knowledge of the terrain to significant effect. The region became an arena of small but intense engagements. The final outcome

---

[75] Hallowed Ground Magazine. (2018, December 18). Revolution on the Frontier. Retrieved from Battlefields.org: https://www.battlefields.org/learn/articles/revolution-frontier.

of operations by both sides in the western frontier was decided by the Treaty of Paris in 1783.

The Road to Yorktown

But before the treaty was signed, there was a pivotal battle in Yorktown. Cornwallis intended to strengthen British control in Virginia. His strategic vision, influenced by the idea of maintaining a southern base for the British forces, led him to choose Yorktown. This coastal town provided a secure port for the British Royal Navy and a defensive position against the threat of French naval interference.

Cornwallis's focus on Virginia was both a response to the shifting dynamics of the war and to perceived weaknesses in the American forces. His strategy was to alter the face of the conflict by bringing the fight to less secure colonial territories, capitalizing on potential loyalist support and drawing the French away from their fleet.

Cornwallis's move to Virginia was risky. It meant a shift from a mobile war that primarily involved raiding and engagements designed to destabilize the American effort to a more static form of warfare. Building a base at Yorktown meant committing troops to a fixed location and inevitably turning it into a target for the combined Franco-American forces. Furthermore, it relied heavily upon the Royal Navy for supplies and evacuation, making the British forces vulnerable to French naval superiority. It would later expose a critical flaw in their strategy once the French fleet took control of Chesapeake Bay.

Washington's Countermove

General George Washington received intelligence of Cornwallis's march to Yorktown in the summer of 1781. Recognizing the strategic implications of this British maneuver, Washington saw an opportunity to strike a decisive blow. In coordination with French General Rochambeau, Washington shifted his focus from the planned attack on New York City to a rapid march toward Virginia. This audacious move, with exceptional secrecy and haste, positioned the Franco-American forces for a surprise assault against Cornwallis's stronghold, effectively trapping the British between their encroaching adversaries and the sea.[76]

The French fleet, commanded by Admiral François de Grasse, was stationed in the West Indies during that summer. De Grasse received

---

[76] History.com Editors. (2023, June 21). Battle of Yorktown. Retrieved from History.com: https://www.history.com/topics/american-revolution/siege-of-yorktown.

dispatches from Washington requesting his urgent arrival to Chesapeake Bay to assist in trapping the British. Understanding the potential impact of his ships, de Grasse promptly set sail for Chesapeake Bay, reaching the Virginian coast by the end of August.

The British navy moved to respond to de Grasse with a fleet of nineteen ships of the line commanded by Admiral Thomas Graves. The French and British fleets fought a pivotal naval engagement on September 5th near the entrance of Chesapeake Bay, now referred to as the Battle of the Capes. The French won the two-hour battle, and the British retreated to New York City.

The French Navy, reinforced by a fleet under the command of Admiral Louis de Barras, now had control of Chesapeake Bay, preventing the British from reinforcing or evacuating Cornwallis's army at Yorktown. Cornwallis was trapped on land without naval support. The British general solidified his defenses by constructing redoubts with artillery support connected by trenches.[77]

Washington's Arrival

Washington and Comte de Rochambeau, the commander of the French troops, arrived in Williamsburg, Virginia, by the middle of September. Their combined force eventually reached over nineteen thousand men. Nine thousand British soldiers opposed them. The siege of Yorktown formally began on September 28th, 1781.[78]

The Siege

The combined American and French forces conducted the siege with methodical precision. The allies dug parallel trenches, bringing artillery and men steadily closer to the British defensive line. Artillery barrages commenced on October 9th, and French cannons pounded British defenses.

The American attack on Redoubt No. 10 was a memorable action during the siege. Under the command of Lieutenant Colonel Alexander Hamilton, a French and American force overran the redoubt on October 14th and secured a crucial foothold in Yorktown's defenses.[79]

[77] NPS.gov. (2021, January 25). Battle of the Capes. Retrieved from Yorktown Battlefield: https://www.nps.gov/york/learn/historyculture/battle-of-the-capes.htm.

[78] Battlefields.org. (2024, February 25). Siege of Yorktown. Retrieved from Battlefields.org: https://www.battlefields.org/learn/revolutionary-war/battles/yorktown.

[79] Battlefields.org. (2024, February 25). Siege of Yorktown. Retrieved from Battlefields.org: https://www.battlefields.org/learn/revolutionary-war/battles/yorktown.

Cornwallis tried to evacuate his troops across the York River on October 16th, but the effort failed. The relief force General Clinton promised him failed to arrive, and the situation was hopeless. A drummer appeared on the British ramparts the morning of October 17th, accompanied by an officer waving a white handkerchief. Lord Cornwallis was ready to negotiate for a surrender.

The Final Surrender

On October 19th, 1781, the siege of Yorktown reached its dramatic conclusion with the formal surrender of General Cornwallis's British forces. The ceremony itself was charged with solemnity and formality. The defeated British soldiers marched out from their positions, laying down their arms in a field cleared for the event. Notably, General Cornwallis claimed illness and sent his second in command, General Charles O'Hara, to offer the British surrender to the American and French commanders.

General Washington remembered the humiliation the Americans were forced to endure at the surrender of Charleston, and he decided to return the favor. He refused a request for a traditional honors of war ceremony and required the defeated to march with flags furled and muskets shouldered. He declined to accept the surrender from O'Hara. Instead, he designated his second in command, General Benjamin Lincoln, who was the defeated American commander at Charleston, to receive the British general's sword. The British surrendered 8,000 men, 214 artillery pieces, and thousands of muskets at Yorktown.

Surrender of Lord Cornwallis by John Trumbull.
https://commons.wikimedia.org/wiki/File:Surrender_of_Lord_Cornwallis.jpg

British Reaction to the Surrender

When news of the defeat at Yorktown reached London, it resounded throughout Parliament and the wider British public. People were shocked, dismayed, and in disbelief. Prime Minister Lord North famously exclaimed, "Oh God! It is all over," as he paced in his room, articulating the sense of finality the loss represented for Britain's efforts to retain control over the American colonies. The political ramifications were immediate, with calls for ending the war and for North's government to resign. The public, weary of the protracted conflict and its economic burdens, began to press for peace. The defeat at Yorktown ended the last vestiges of popular and political support for the war in Great Britain.

The victory at Yorktown effectively ended major combat operations in North America, setting the stage for the negotiation of the Treaty of Paris and the formal recognition of the United States' independence by the British Crown. The Americans had done the improbable and achieved the impossible.

Chapter 12: The Final Days

The surrender at Yorktown was not the end of the American Revolution, but it was the beginning of the end. What happened in the following months created the blueprint for the United States of America. The most significant work was done thousands of miles from the North American battlefields.

<u>The Treaty of Paris</u>

The negotiations that led to the Treaty of Paris began with the appointment of a special commission from the United States. Benjamin Franklin, John Adams, and John Jay were charged with representing American interests in talks with the British. (The original group included Thomas Jefferson and Henry Laurens. Jefferson was unable to leave America, and Laurens was a prisoner in the Tower of London.) They arrived in Europe amidst the endgame of a war that both sides wanted to be over and done with.

The earl of Shelburne, who led British negotiations, was a politician known for his forward-thinking stance on colonial autonomy. Assisting him were Richard Oswald, a businessman who understood transatlantic business affairs, and Henry Strachey, an experienced secretary who would become instrumental in articulating the treaty's details. Together, the British trio engaged with their American counterparts in complex discussions that navigated various diplomatic challenges to ultimately define the peace terms between the two nations.

The commissioners found themselves navigating a treacherous sea of European politics. Britain, smarting from the loss of the American colonies, was not the only player at this table. France, a critical ally in the American Revolution, had its own agenda. France sought to weaken its rival, Great Britain, while ensuring the repayment of debts owed by America and maintaining its territorial holdings in the Caribbean. On the other hand, Spain was focused on securing control over Florida, which it had captured from Britain during the war, and protecting its colonies in Central and South America from future American expansion. The American commissioners participated in a delicate dance to ensure that the treaty negotiated with the British did not compromise their relations with the French, Spanish, or other European powers.[80]

The meetings began in the spring of 1782 and were held in Paris. Significant issues that dominated the Treaty of Paris discussions were the recognition of the United States as an independent sovereign free from British rule and the possession of territories, boundaries, and fisheries. Although Great Britain would have to swallow its pride, formal recognition of America as an independent country was a non-negotiable.

A Question of Boundaries

The war on the western frontier was a primary factor in the boundary issues. Hostilities between American frontier settlers and Native American tribes, backed at times by British forces, had become an integral part of the conflict. The United States sought to establish secure and recognized boundaries that would allow for westward expansion and the development of new states. The British held a series of forts in the Great Lakes region, which they were reluctant to abandon. They hoped to maintain a buffer zone to protect their fur trade interests and relations with various Native American tribes. The American commissioners pushed the British to relinquish their forts and any claims to territory east of the Mississippi River, ensuring a clear path for America's growth.[81]

Bargaining over Seafood

Discussions over fisheries may appear trivial to modern society, but these patches of watery real estate held immense economic and strategic importance. The abundant fishing grounds along the coast of Newfoundland and in the Gulf of Saint Lawrence were a vital source of

[80] History.com. (2023, June 21). Treaty of Paris. Retrieved from History.com: https://www.history.com/topics/american-revolution/treaty-of-paris.
[81] Ruppert, B. (2016, August 4). How Article 7 Freed 3000 Slaves. Retrieved from Allthingsliberty.com: https://allthingsliberty.com/2016/08/how-article-7-freed-3000-slaves/.

livelihood for many American fishermen and a cornerstone of commerce for the northeast. British recognition of American fishing rights was a non-negotiable element for the American delegates, as it would secure a prosperous and strategically valuable industry for the newly independent nation.[82]

What to Do with the Loyalists

For the British, offering protection to the loyalists was an obligation of honor to those who had supported Great Britain's cause and a reflection of its commitment to its subjects. Assurances for their safety and compensation for their losses were vital in maintaining the British Crown's honor and forestalling future insurrections within the rest of the empire.

The Final Copy

Through skillful negotiation and strategic maneuvering, the commissioners crafted a treaty that would shape the future of their respective nations. The recognition of American independence was a watershed moment, laying to rest any lingering doubts about the permanence of the new nation. The delineation of boundaries, most notably the extension of the United States to the Mississippi River, set the stage for westward expansion and the acquisition of vast territories.

The treaty also provided for the British evacuation of their forces from the United States, marking the end of a military occupation that had long outstayed its welcome. In return, the Americans agreed to ensure property restitution to loyalists and take steps to prevent further seizure or harm.

Great Britain dealt with the American allies in separate agreements. France regained territories in the Caribbean occupied by the British, fortifying its foothold in the region. Spain regained Florida, which it had lost to the British during the Seven Years' War, and it also secured the expansion of its territory in North America, including control over the strategically important port of New Orleans. These gains were critical to Spain's objective of reinforcing its colonial empire and securing a buffer against future American expansion.[83]

---

[82] Cronin, A. (2015, April 3). Untangling North Atlantic Fishing, 1764-1910 Part 2: Anglo-American Treaties Regarding the Fishery, 1783-1818. Retrieved from Massit.org: https://www.masshist.org/beehiveblog/2015/04/untangling-north-atlantic-fishing-1764-1910-part-2-anglo-american-treaties-regarding-the-fishery-1783-1818/.

[83] Famguardian.org. (2024, February 26). The Definitive Treaty of Paris 1783. Retrieved from

The Treaty of Paris was signed by the American and British delegates on September 3rd, 1783, and formally ended the American Revolutionary War. The Continental Congress ratified it on January 14th, 1784, and Great Britain did the same on April 9th, 1784.

<u>The Last Days: The Newburgh Conspiracy</u>

There were still hostilities as the Treaty of Paris was being negotiated. The fighting between the Americans and the Native Americans on the western frontier was intense. However, the fighting was winding down since everyone knew peace was being ironed out. Nobody wanted to be the last person to die in the war.

There was a mutiny of Continental soldiers in Pennsylvania because of back pay issues. It was put down quickly by a contingent of 1,500 soldiers sent by Washington. A noteworthy dissent was the Newburgh Conspiracy. Once again, back pay was an issue.

Many officers of the Continental Army were on the cusp of open revolt. Their discontent stemmed from Congress's indecision on whether to honor its promise to pay the war veterans and the belief that their sacrifices for the cause of independence were being disregarded. Those stationed at Newburgh, New York, were deeply worried that the Continental Congress would not honor its obligations, including pensions, to those who had risked their lives for the new nation. A memorandum composed of officers led by Henry Knox was sent to Congress in December 1782, expressing frustration over the issues of back pay in arrears and pensions. The Continental Congress discussed the issue, but the primary problem was that there was no money to fund the demands. That admission only made things worse.

A letter reportedly written by Major John Armstrong circulated in the Newburgh camp, stating that the army should disband before the peace treaty was signed unless their demands were met. The possibility of a military coup d'état was implicit in the letter. Despite Washington's opposition, a meeting of all officers was called for on March 11th, 1783. Washington asked the officers to wait four days before they met to allow tempers to cool. The officers' meeting was held on March 15th. To everyone's surprise, General Washington entered the room and asked to be allowed to speak. The commander in chief knew that a full-scale

Fanguardian.org:
https://fanguardian.org/PublishedAuthors/Govt/USTreaties/DefinitiveTreatyOfPeace1783.pdf.

mutiny could happen and made the most of his time.[84]

Washington appealed to their sense of honor, patriotism, and shared struggle, urging them to give the government time to make good on its promises. Washington's words were a heartfelt call to the ideals and values upon which the nation was being founded. He emphasized that the very essence of the republic for which they fought hinged on subordination to civilian authority and denounced any actions that would undermine the fragile roots of American democracy. Washington's address was a masterful blend of persuasion and leadership, dissuading his officers from taking a path that could irrevocably alter the course of the young republic.[85]

George Washington was a father figure to these officers. His emotional pleas stirred these men who had watched the general share their sufferings and bear the burden of command for years. Many wept. The officers resolved to respect the wishes of their commander. The bond that Washington had worked to build with his officers made the difference.

Final Days: The New York Evacuation

The departure of thirty thousand British soldiers from New York City was not merely a military maneuver; it set off a chain reaction that reshaped the political, social, and economic fabric of the fledgling United States. On November 25th, 1783, the British began their evacuation. With hundreds of ships, the British ferried their men, equipment, and loyalist supporters out of the city to the waiting vessels in the harbor.

The process was not without its complications; disputes over the protection of loyalists and the logistics of the withdrawal posed significant challenges. Yet, the retreat was mostly peaceful, and the transition of power to the newly independent United States was underway.

Integral to the complexity of the evacuation was the fate of the loyalists. It was a topic of heated debate during the peace negotiations

---

[84] Hattem, M. (2024, February 26). Newburgh Conspiracy. Retrieved from Mountvernon.org: https://www.mountvernon.org/library/digitalhistory/digital-encyclopedia/article/newburgh-conspiracy/.
[85] Washington, G. (2024, February 26). Newburgh Address: George Washington to Officers of the Army, March 15, 1783. Retrieved from MountVernon.org: https://www.mountvernon.org/education/primary-source-collections/primary-source-collections/article/newburgh-address-george-washington-to-officers-of-the-army-march-15-1783/.

and remained a point of contention until the last moment of the withdrawal. The British assured safe passage to loyalists who chose to leave with them. Those who did not leave faced an uncertain and often hostile reception from their former countrymen.

Estimates suggest that thousands of loyalists were evacuated from New York City alongside the British troops. Their departure led them to various destinations, primarily other parts of the British Empire, where they sought safety and the chance to rebuild their lives. Many sailed to the Canadian provinces of Nova Scotia and New Brunswick, which the British government had prepared to receive them. Others found refuge in Quebec, Ontario, and Prince Edward Island, while many others relocated to Britain or other British colonies in the West Indies. This large-scale migration forged new communities and impacted the demographics and cultures of the areas where loyalists settled.

The Departure of African Americans

On the docks of New York City at the time of the evacuation, there were chaotic scenes similar to what happened at the fall of Saigon in 1975 and the evacuation of Kabaul in 2021. A palpable sense of urgency gripped the African American population in New York City, particularly those who had escaped slavery and fought for the Crown. The promise of freedom was within reach, yet the chaos and uncertainty of the evacuation sparked fear of recapture and re-enslavement by American forces. They had reason to be concerned.

The Treaty of Paris included an unprecedented article in international law: Article 7. This provision, championed by the American negotiators, stipulated that the British would return any slaves belonging to Americans "in whatever part of the world British forces might occupy." This meant that those who were once slaves and had escaped to the British lines might be returned to their former owners.[86]

The British military commanders, recognizing the dedication and contributions of these individuals to their cause, felt an obligation to honor the promise of freedom that was given in exchange for service.

To facilitate the safe passage of those former slaves who had served the Crown, the British meticulously documented their names in the "Book of Negroes," a ledger that served as a form of protection and

[86] Ruppert, B. (2016, August 4). How Article 7 Freed 3000 Slaves. Retrieved from Allthingsliberty.com: https://allthingsliberty.com/2016/08/how-article-7-freed-3000-slaves/.

legitimacy for their evacuation. This level of record-keeping provided a loophole, allowing the British to argue that these individuals had earned their freedom through service rather than being considered property that needed to be returned to American slaveholders. The information allowed the runaway slaves to be evacuated alongside British forces as they were transported to British territories. It is believed around nine thousand African Americans left with the British.[87]

The question of slavery could not be swept under the carpet forever. It eventually resulted in a war that would kill hundreds of thousands.

The evacuation of New York City marked the dawn of a new era for the United States. Americans were no longer the subjects of the British Crown. They were now part of a new nation that had unique challenges and obstacles to overcome.

[87] Tsaltas-Ottomanelli, L. G. (2023, November 15). Black Loyalists in the Evacuation of New York City, 1783. Retrieved from Gothamcenter.org: https://www.gothamcenter.org/blog/black-loyalists-evaculation-zv4la.

Conclusion

The American Revolution shook the world and introduced a period of change that lasted well into the 19th century. No one expected the Americans to take on the British and win, but it happened.

Some history lessons learned from the American Revolution are worth considering today. The Fabian battle strategy worked. Washington and Greene avoided an enemy with superior numbers and fought another day numerous times. They sometimes lost, but they often inflicted serious damage on the British anyway, so any victory was expensive. Interestingly, many British officers were very familiar with classical history. The generals overlooked a strategy that permitted the Romans to defeat Hannibal.

Arrogance and pride do come before the fall. The British Parliament had many opportunities to be reasonable and negotiate with the dissatisfied colonists. The Americans were willing to stay a part of the British Empire until the Olive Branch Petition failed. Consequently, they decided they had no choice but to declare independence and go their separate ways. The British government was too proud to admit it was wrong on occasions when Parliament was taking the wrong path. Parliament should have listened to people like Edmund Burke but didn't. The British paid dearly for not listening to wise counsel.

Courage wins battles, but persistence wins wars. The American Continental Army could have disbanded after several battles, but it did not. Instead, the patriots stuck together and stayed the course. Valley Forge is a striking example of perseverance under enormous hardship.

The Americans believed in a cause and were prepared to continue the struggle.

The United States of America continues to be a positive example to other nations. Liberty is a cause worth fighting for, and Americans in the American Revolutionary War put their lives on the line for the right to be free. That struggle and the common people's fight for their rights is something that all Americans can justifiably be proud of.

If you enjoyed this book, a review on Amazon would be greatly appreciated because it would mean a lot to hear from you.

To leave a review:

1. Open your camera app.
2. Point your mobile device at the QR code.
3. The review page will appear in your web browser.

Thanks for your support!

Here's another book by Enthralling History that you might like

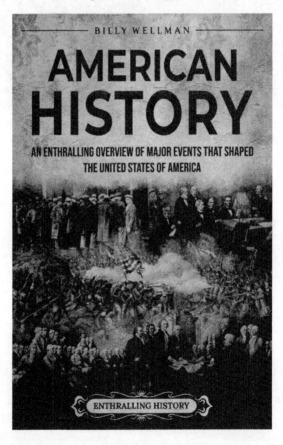

Free limited time bonus

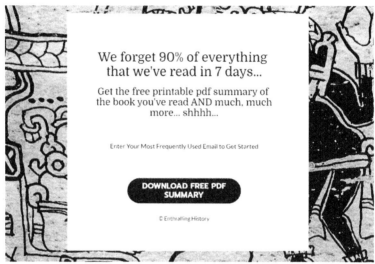

Stop for a moment. We have a free bonus set up for you. The problem is this: we forget 90% of everything that we read after 7 days. Crazy fact, right? Here's the solution: we've created a printable, 1-page pdf summary for this book that you're reading now. All you have to do to get your free pdf summary is to go to the following website: https://livetolearn.lpages.co/enthrallinghistory/

Or, Scan the QR code!

Once you do, it will be intuitive. Enjoy, and thank you!

Bibliography

American Battlefield Trust. (2024, February 15). Bunker Hill. Retrieved from Battlefields.org: https://www.battlefields.org/learn/revolutionary-war/battles/bunker-hill.

American Battlefield Trust. (2024, February 15). Fort Ticonderoga, May 10, 1775. Retrieved from American Battlefield Trust: https://www.battlefields.org/learn/maps/fort-ticonderoga-may-10-1775.

American History Central. (2024, February 10). The Suffolk Resolves. Americanhistorycentral.com. Retrieved from Suffolk Resolves Summary 1774: https://www.americanhistorycentral.com/entries/suffolk-resolves/.

American History Central. (2024, February 4). The Navigation Acts. Retrieved from Americanhistorycentral.com: https://www.americanhistorycentral.com/entries/navigation-acts/.

Battlefields.org. (2024, February 20). Waxhaws. Retrieved from Battlefields.org: https://www.battlefields.org/learn/revolutionary-war/battles/waxhaws.

Battlefields.org. (2024, January 23). 10 Facts: The Continental Army. Retrieved from Battlefields.org: https://www.battlefields.org/learn/articles/10-facts-continental-army.

Battlefields.org. (2024, February 21). Brandywine. Retrieved from Batlefields.org: https://www.battlefields.org/learn/revolutionary-war/battles/brandywine.

Battlefields.org. (2024, February 20). Camden. Retrieved from Batlefields.org: https://www.battlefields.org/learn/revolutionary-war/battles/camden.

Battlefields.org. (2024, February 21). Germantown. Retrieved from Battlefields.org: https://www.battlefields.org/learn/revolutionary-war/battles/germantown.

Battlefields.org. (2024, February 20). Horatio Gates. Retrieved from Battlefields.org: https://www.battlefields.org/learn/biographies/horatio-gates

Battlefields.org. (2024, February 20). Siege of Savannah. Retrieved from Battlefields.org: https://www.battlefields.org/learn/revolutionary-war/battles/savannah.

Battlefields.org. (2024, February 25). Siege of Yorktown. Retrieved from Battlefields.org: https://www.battlefields.org/learn/revolutionary-war/battles/yorktown.

BBC.com. (2024, February 17). Philosophers Justifying Slavery. Retrieved from Ethics guide: https://www.bbc.co.uk/ethics/slavery/ethics/philosophers_1.shtml.

Bill of Rights Institute. (2024, February 17). Thomas Jefferson and the Declaration of Independence. Retrieved from Billofrightsinstitute.org: https://billofrightsinstitute.org/essays/thomas-jefferson-and-the-declaration-of-independence.

Bill, R. (2021, August 4). The Northern Campaign of 1777. Retrieved from Nps.gov: https://www.nps.gov/fost/blogs/the-northern-campaign-of-1777.htm.

Boston National Historical Park. (2024, February 15). Dorchester Heights. Retrieved from Nps.org: https://www.nps.gov/places/dorchester-heights.htm.

Boston National Historical Park. (2024, February 11). Samuel Adams: Boston's Radical Revolutionary. Retrieved from National Park Service: https://www.nps.gov/articles/000/samuel-adams-boston-revolutionary.htm

BritishBattles.com. (2024, February 14). Battle of Lexington and Concord. Retrieved from Britishbattles.com: https://www.britishbattles.com/war-of-the-revolution-1775-to-1783/battle-of-lexington-and-concord/.

Colonial Williamsburg. (2024, February 11). William Pitt's Defense of the American Colonies. Retrieved from Slaveryandrembrance.org: https://www.slaveryandremembrance.org/Almanack/life/politics/pitt.cfm.

Cronin, A. (2015, April 3). Untangling North Atlantic Fishing, 1764-1910 Part 2: Anglo-American Treaties Regarding the Fishery, 1783-1818. Retrieved from Massit.org: https://www.masshist.org/beehiveblog/2015/04/untangling-north-atlantic-fishing-1764-1910-part-2-anglo-american-treaties-regarding-the-fishery-1783-1818/.

Editors, H. (2024, February 21). British Abandon Philadelphia. Retrieved from History.com: https://www.history.com/this-day-in-history/british-abandon-philadelphia.

Eisenhuth, C. (2024, February 10). The Coercive (Intolerable) Acts of 1774. Retrieved from Mountvernon.org: https://www.mountvernon.org/library/digitalhistory/digital-encyclopedia/article/the-coercive-intolerable-acts-of-1774/#:~:text=The%20Coercive%20Acts%20were%20meant,particular%20aspect%20of%20colonial%20life.

Ellis, J. J. (2024, February 4). John Adams. Retrieved from Britannica.com: https://www.britannica.com/biography/John-Adams-president-of-United-States.

Encyclopedia.com. (2024, January 30). Franco-American Alliance. Retrieved from Britannica.com: https://www.britannica.com/event/Franco-American-Alliance

Famguardian.org. (2024, February 26). The Definitive Treaty of Paris 1783. Retrieved from Fanguardian.org: https://famguardian.org/PublishedAuthors/Govt/USTreaties/DefinitiveTreatyOfPeace1783.pdf.

Founders Online. (2024, February 10). The Final Hearing. Retrieved from Founders Online: https://founders.archives.gov/documents/Franklin/01-21-02-0018.

Franklin, Benjamin. (2024, February 10). Benjamin Franklin in His Own Words. Retrieved from Loc.gov: https://www.loc.gov/exhibits/franklin/franklin-break.html.

Hallowed Ground Magazine. (2018, December 18). Revolution on the Frontier. Retrieved from Battefields.org: https://www.battlefields.org/learn/articles/revolution-frontier.

Hattem, M. (2024, February 26). Newburgh Conspiracy. Retrieved from Mountvernon.org: https://www.mountvernon.org/library/digitalhistory/digital-encyclopedia/article/newburgh-conspiracy/.

Hickman, K. (2019, June 13). American Revolution: General Thomas Gage. Retrieved from Thoughtco.com: https://www.thoughtco.com/general-thomas-gage-2360620.

History.com. (2023, June 21). Treaty of Paris. Retrieved from History.com: https://www.history.com/topics/american-revolution/treaty-of-paris.

History.com. (2024, February 21). George Washington Crosses the Delaware. Retrieved from History.com: https://www.history.com/this-day-in-history/washington-crosses-the-delaware.

History.com Editors. (2009, October 27). Boston Tea Party. Retrieved from History.com: https://www.history.com/topics/american-revolution/boston-tea-party.

History.com Editors. (2009, June 13). Townshend Acts. Retrieved from History.com: https://www.history.com/topics/american-revolution/townshend-acts.

History.com Editors. (2023, June 21). Battle of Yorktown. Retrieved from History.com: https://www.history.com/topics/american-revolution/siege-of-yorktown.

History.com Editors. (2024, February 11). British Parliament Passes Unpopular Tea Act. Retrieved from History.com: https://www.history.com/this-day-in-history/parliament-passes-the-tea-act.

Horan, Katherine. (2024, February 10). First Continental Congress. Retrieved from Mountvernon.org: https://www.mountvernon.org/library/digitalhistory/digital-encyclopedia/article/first-continental-congress/#:~:text=One%20of%20the%20Congress%27s%20first,and%20to%20raise%20a%20militia.

Howe, W. (2024, February 1). William Howe Goes His Own Way. Retrieved from Clements.umoich.edu: https://clements.umich.edu/exhibit/spy-letters-of-the-american-revolution/stories-of-spies/howe-goes-his-own-way/.

Hurst, N. T. (2020, March 17). Made in American. Retrieved from Colonialwilliamsburg.org: https://www.colonialwilliamsburg.org/trend-tradition-magazine/spring-2018/made-american/.

Jstor.org. (2024, February 18). Foreign Intervention ... in the American Revolution. Retrieved from Jstor.org: https://daily.jstor.org/intervention-american-revolution/.

Keesling, D. K. (2024, February 21). Valley Forge: A Place of Transformation for the Continental Army. Retrieved from Thepursuitofhistory.org: https://thepursuitofhistory.org/2022/10/24/valley-forge-a-place-of-transformation-for-the-continental-army/.

Kiger, P. J. (2023, July 11). How Thomas Paine's "Common Sense" Helped Inspire the American Revolution. Retrieved from History.com: https://www.history.com/news/thomas-paine-common-sense-revolution.

Lee Resolution (2022, February 8). Lee Resolution. Retrieved from National Archives: https://www.archives.gov/milestone-documents/lee-resolution.

Longley, R. (2020, October 14). Committees of Correspondence: Definition and History. Retrieved from Thoughtco.com: https://www.thoughtco.com/committees-of-correspondence-definition-and-history-5082089.

Makos, I. (2021, April 13). Roles of Native Americans during the American Revolution. Retrieved from Battlefields.org:

https://www.battlefields.org/learn/articles/roles-native-americans-during-revolution.

Maloy, M. (2024, February 21). The Battle of Freeman's Farm: September 19, 1777. Retrieved from Battlefields.org: https://www.battlefields.org/learn/articles/battle-freemans-farm-september-19-1777.

Mark, H. W. (2024, January 25). Battle of Long Island. Retrieved from Worldhistory.com: https://www.worldhistory.org/article/2359/battle-of-long-island/.

Mark, H. W. (2024, February 1). New York and New Jersey Campaign. Retrieved from Worldhistory.com: https://www.worldhistory.org/article/2364/new-york-and-new-jersey-campaign/.

Mary Stockwell, P. (2024, February 21). Baron Von Steuben. Retrieved from Mountvernon.org: https://www.mountvernon.org/library/digitalhistory/digital-encyclopedia/article/baron-von-steuben/.

massmoments.org. (2024, February 15). Henry Knox Brings Cannon to Boston. Retrieved from massmoments.org: https://www.massmoments.org/moment-details/henry-knox-brings-cannon-to-boston.html.

McGee, S. (2023, August 25). 5 Ways the French Helped Win the American Revolution. Retrieved from History.com: https://www.history.com/news/american-revolution-french-role-help.

Mobley, C. (2006, September 24). Hundreds of African-Americans Campaigned for the King during 1779 Struggle for Savannah. Retrieved from Savannahnow.com: https://www.savannahnow.com/story/news/2006/09/25/hundreds-african-americans-campaigned-king-during-1779-struggle-savannah/13826035007/.

Mount Vernon. (2024, February 11). The Coercive (Intolerable) Acts of 1774. Retrieved from Mountvernon.org: https://www.mountvernon.org/library/digitalhistory/digital-encyclopedia/article/the-coercive-intolerable-acts-of-1774/#:~:text=The%20Coercive%20Acts%20were%20meant,particular%20aspect%20of%20colonial%20life.

Mountvernon.org. (2024, February 21). 10 Facts About Washington's Crossing of the Delaware River. Retrieved from George Washington's Mount Vernon: https://www.mountvernon.org/george-washington/the-revolutionary-war/washingtons-revolutionary-war-battles/the-trenton-princeton-campaign/10-facts-about-washingtons-crossing-of-the-delaware-river/.

Museum of the American Revolution. (2024, February 18). Spain and the American Revolution. Retrieved from Amrevmuseum.org:

https://www.amrevmuseum.org/spain-and-the-american-revolution.

National Geographic. (2024, February 17). Signing of the Declaration of Independence. Retrieved from Education.nationalgeographic.org: https://education.nationalgeographic.org/resource/signing-declaration-independence/.

National Park Service. (2024, February 18). The Clinton-Sullivan Campaign of 1779. Retrieved from Nps.gov: https://www.nps.gov/articles/000/the-clinton-sullivan-campaign-of-1779.htm.

National Park Service. (2024, February 21). Henry Clinton. Retrieved from Nps.gov: https://www.nps.gov/people/henry-clinton.htm#:~:text=Sir%20Henry%20Clinton%20replaced%20Sir,to%20face%20the%20rebellious%20Americans.

NCC Staff. (2021, May 24). 10 Fascinating Facts About John Hancock. Retrieved from Constitutioncenter.org: https://constitutioncenter.org/blog/10-fascinating-facts-about-john-hancock.

NPS.gov. (2021, January 25). Battle of the Capes. Retrieved from Yorktown Battlefield: https://www.nps.gov/york/learn/historyculture/battle-of-the-capes.htm.

Orrison, R. (2024, January 3). Native American Impact on British War Strategy in Southern Campaign. Retrieved from Battlefields.org: https://www.battlefields.org/learn/articles/native-american-impact-british-war-strategy-southern-campaign.

Oxford Learning Link. (2024, February 11). Document-Edmund Burke, Excerpts from "Conciliation with the Colonies." Retrieved from Learnnglink.oup.com: https://learninglink.oup.com/access/content/schaller-3e-dashboard-resources/document-edmund-burke-excerpts-from-conciliation-with-the-colonies-1775.

Paine, T. (2024, February 17). Thomas Paine, Common Sense, 1776. Retrieved from Billofrightsinstitute.org: https://billofrightsinstitute.org/activities/thomas-paine-common-sense-1776.

Paine, T. (1776). The American Crisis. Retrieved from Library of Congress: https://www.loc.gov/resource/cph.3b06889/.

Powell, J. (1996, September 1). Charles James Fox, Valiant Voice for Liberty. Retrieved from Foundation for Economic Freedom: https://fee.org/articles/charles-james-fox-valiant-voice-for-liberty/.

Revolutionarywar.us. (2024, February 21). Southern Theater. Retrieved from Revolutionarywar.us: https://revolutionarywar.us/campaigns/1775-1782-southern-theater/.

Revolutionarywar.us. (2024, February 21). The Battle of Kings Mountain. Retrieved from Revolutionarywar.us: https://revolutionarywar.us/year-1780/battle-kings-mountain/.

Revolutionary-war-and-beyond.com. (2024, February 24). Admiral Howe's Fleet Arrives at Staten Island. Retrieved from Revolutionary-war-and-beyond.com: https://www.revolutionary-war-and-beyond.com/admiral-howes-fleet-arrives-staten-island.html.

Rosenfield, R. (2024, February 21). Princeton. Retrieved from Battlefields.org: https://www.battlefields.org/learn/articles/princeton.

Ruppert, B. (2016, August 4). How Article 7 Freed 3000 Slaves. Retrieved from Allthingsliberty.com: https://allthingsliberty.com/2016/08/how-article-7-freed-3000-slaves/.

Rust, R. (2023, April 14). The Powder Alarm of Massachusetts in 1774. Retrieved from Americanhistorycentral.com: https://www.americanhistorycentral.com/entries/powder-alarm-1774-massachusetts/.

Scythes, J. (2024, February 21). Conway Cabal. Retrieved from Mountvernon.org: https://www.mountvernon.org/library/digitalhistory/digital-encyclopedia/article/conway-cabal/#:~:text=The%20Conway%20Cabal%20refers%20to,with%20Major%20General%20Horatio%20Gates.

Sprague, D. (2023, January 24). American Revolution and Canada. Retrieved from Thecanadianencyclopedia.ca: https://www.thecanadianencyclopedia.ca/en/article/american-revolution.

The Paul Revere House. (2024, February 14). The Real Story of Paul Revere's Ride. Retrieved from Paulreverehouse.org: https://www.paulreverehouse.org/the-real-story/.

Triber, J. E. (2024, February 4). Britain Begins Taxing the Colonies: The Sugar & Stamp Acts. Retrieved from Nos.gov: https://www.nps.gov/articles/000/sugar-and-stamp-acts.htm.

Tsaltas-Ottomanelli, L. G. (2023, November 15). Black Loyalists in the Evacuation of New York City, 1783. Retrieved from Gothamcenter.org: https://www.gothamcenter.org/blog/black-loyalists-evaculation-zy4la.

UKessays.com. (2024, February 17). Aristotle's Views on Slavery. Retrieved from UKessays.com: https://www.ukessays.com/essays/politics/slavery.php.

Washington, G. (2024, February 26). Newburgh Address: George Washington to Officers of the Army, March 15, 1783. Retrieved from MountVernon.org: https://www.mountvernon.org/education/primary-source-collections/primary-source-collections/article/newburgh-address-george-washington-to-officers-of-the-army-march-15-1783/.

Wigington, P. (2018, November 29). What Were the Navigation Acts? Retrieved from Thoughtco.com: https://www.thoughtco.com/navigation-acts-4177756.

William P. Kladky, P. (2024, February 15). Continental Army. Retrieved from Mountvernon.org: https://www.mountvernon.org/library/digitalhistory/digital-encyclopedia/article/continental-army/.

Wirt, William (ed. 1973). Give Me Liberty or Give Me Death. Retrieved from Colonial Williamsburg: https://www.colonialwilliamsburg.org/learn/deep-dives/give-me-liberty-or-give-me-death/.

Zeidan, A. (2024, February 4). Stamp Act Congress. Retrieved from Britannica.com: https://www.britannica.com/topic/Stamp-Act-Congress.

Zielinski, A. E. (2021, November 17). What Was the Stamp Act Congress and Why Did It Matter. Retrieved from Ameicanbattlefields.org: https://www.battlefields.org/learn/articles/what-was-stamp-act-congress.

Printed in Great Britain
by Amazon

47691636R00086